The

Great Shift

The
Great Shift

CO-CREATING A NEW WORLD
for 2012 AND BEYOND

FEATURING Lee Carroll & Kryon,
Tom Kenyon & The Hathors & Mary Magdalen,
Particia Cori & The High Council of Sirius

EDITED BY Martine Vallée

WEISERBOOKS
San Francisco, CA / Newburyport, MA

First published in 2009 by
Red Wheel/Weiser, LLC
With offices at:
500 Third Street, Suite 230
San Francisco, CA 94107
www.redwheelweiser.com

ISBN: 978-1-57863-457-6
Library of Congress Cataloging-in-Publication Data available upon request.

Cover and text design by Tracy Johnson
Typeset in Garamond and Futura
Cover photograph © 2008 Lexx/istockphoto

Printed in Canada
TCP
10 9 8 7 6 5 4 3 2 1

CONTENTS

INTRODUCTION

A warm welcome to all of you. First and foremost, I want to thank you for taking the time to read this information. Being in the publishing business for fifteen years, I see all the books that are available and the extraordinary number of choices that you have. Never has there been so much information available on every subject imaginable, in every form possible. So to pick up a book is really a conscious decision and I am very grateful for the time that you are taking from your busy schedule to read what I have to offer.

To say how thrilled I am to see this book in a language other than the original French is an understatement. I am so grateful to everyone at Weiser Books and in particular to Jan Johnson, for following her intuition and going ahead with this project. If it was not for her, you would not be reading this.

Having published some great authors myself over the years, each of them sharing their inspired information in many languages for the benefit of readers everywhere, I thought that the time had come to reunite some of them in one unique literary project. What you are about to read is the result of such a gathering, with no other purpose than to bring a better understanding of what is going on not only inside us but also all around us. The point is to better deal with what we are all feeling at some level or the other.

You'll hear from three great authors in this volume. First you have Lee Carroll/Kryon, whose work through *The Kryon Writings* is surely one of the most credible information that exists right now. I've been publishing his information since 1996. I must admit that for me, it was love at first sight. I first came across Kryon/Lee at a new age event in New York. I was so captivated by these writings that I read the first book in its entirety, sitting on a chair in the hotel lobby. I knew then that Kryon and his teaching were to change my life and the lives of my readers. Over the years, Lee Carroll has became a very good friend. We have travelled on many occasions together and he still comes to Montreal to do events every two years. He is a man that I admire deeply for his devotion to his work and for the manner in which he does it. It is an honor to publish his work and have him as a friend.

Tom Kenyon is also a very special man with so many talents. I heard about him before I even read any of his information. Finally, in September 2007, another of my authors, Drunvalo Melchizedek, told me "You must meet Tom Kenyon." Then, two or three months later, a lady named Wendy came into my office and asked me to publish Tom and Judi's book *The Magdalen Manuscript.* I did, and felt very strongly that they had to be part of *The Great Shift.* Tom channels information from Mary Magdalen and The Hathors. From what I know, very few people are as devoted to bringing back the divine feminine as Tom and Judi are, and I admire them greatly for their devotion to this mission. Lastly, you have Patricia Cori, who works with the Sirian High Council. She is a pioneer and has published many books already, all of great interest. She is a wonderful woman, in complete service to humanity.

Inspiration is always something very unique and amazing, and it brings many surprises along its path. You know it's beginning but never its end. When I first began exploring the idea of creating this series, it was simply because I wanted my readers to be able to navigate more easily the energies bringing us closer to the 2012 marker that everybody is talking about. We have so many expectations about 2012 . . . but we have to get there first. If there is something that I know for certain, it is that we won't get there in the same bodies that we started with, and we won't get there with the same belief system that we once had. These are some of the reasons why it is so difficult for so many at this time. We have to let the changes happen because if we don't, by the time 2012 rings our doorbell, we will be exhausted from so much resistance. That's the reason behind this book: To help you better understand and face these changes that every human being is feeling, consciously or not, but at some level or the other.

No doubt, there a shift going on, not only in ourselves but in every country and in every culture. It's huge and it is everywhere. It is changing us at the most profound level and thus creating such a grand movement of compassion that it cannot be denied anymore. Everywhere people are awakening and changing the direction of their lives and speaking their truth. But this great shift comes with a great challenge—our ego. He's trying very hard to keep us entrenched in the illusion of whom we are not, instead of who we are. Becoming conscious of the ego is the first step to freedom from fear and toward peace of mind. But to do that we have to become conscious of how our ego works. You see, our soul is always looking for a way to shine its light through us. It could happen through meditation, through compassion, with a workshop, by expressing our talents through the arts, or by a simple walk in nature. If we chose to live consciously by nourishing our soul and not our ego, we would all have a passionate life. And with passion comes creativity, what I call the "fire within."

I read this once about the ego: There is a big difference between living our life through the light of our soul or through the deceptive light of the ego. It is easy to be fooled, because the ego is subtle but at the same time strong and deceitful. If we pay close attention, it is very easy to see how the ego, when threatended, tries to darken our true light by sending us on a false path. I think that our progress is directly proportional to our capacity to eliminate the ego and our tendencies for drama as much as possible: To go from ME to WE. Changing our perspective about who we are will change the world we live in.

So here we are again, on this never-ending journey between light and darkness, courage and fear, being the change we want to see or being scared of what might happen if we do. But if we are willing to take the next step, we will discover that there is only one light, one journey, one family. Nobel Peace prize winner Desmond Tutu once said, "One day, we will wake up and realize that we are all family." We are so close to seeing that happen.

To each one of you I say this: love each other, be at peace in your heart, and always try to live by your truth. Then your life will be lived through the light of who you really are—and that will make a difference in the world. That is what the great shift is all about.

Martine Vallée
Montreal, Quebec, Canada
martinevallee@qc.aira.com

Part One

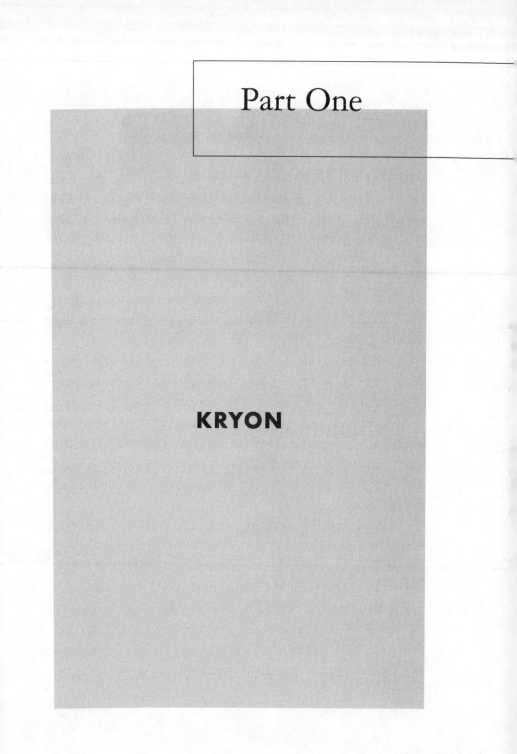

KRYON

INTRODUCTION FROM LEE CARROLL

This introduction is going to be about the director of this book, Martine Vallée.

Martine never could have conceived that she might change thousands of lives. For years she hid behind the cloak of what was given to her within her culture and her circumstances. For years she considered herself only in the light that others gave her to look at, not the light that came from her own magnificence. For most of her life she walked as most of us did, in the groove of an existence we thought we could not change or control.

I want the readers to know that I've known her for many years, and saw her take her power. For she is an example of what Kryon teaches, in that she overcame what her circumstances created for her, and instead began to co-create her own reality! Through intent and integrity, she began to let her light shine in a fashion that changed the energy of her life. Her work has highlighted profound truth in the lives of thousands of people.

One woman, like so many others at this time, decided to find her purpose and to lift herself out of darkness, into a light that was created by her own Higher-Self. The rest is history, and the book you are looking at is a series, intuitively designed and created by her, for you. It was originally published in French and now available in English for the first time. Take a look at the content and celebrate the truth within it, as it continues to change lives.

This is what we teach . . . that no matter who you are on the planet, your decisions to find the God inside you can result in magnificent things. That is what the great shift is all about.

FROM KRYON

Greetings, Dear Ones, I am Kryon of Magnetic service.

Once again you open these pages expecting to receive something that would represent a communication from the other side of the veil. However, it's time to start melding our two energies in a much more profound way.

The Humans who grace these pages with their eyes have something in common: They are coming together in unity to give you a combined message in love. Most of them don't know each other, and never will see each other, yet the "voice" that comes through them represents a single message of love. This is not a communication from entities who are foreign to you, but rather an enhancement of the sweet voice that is already in your head that you were born with. It's the connection to family, and the Higher-Self that we all represent. Rather than an odd esoteric message from "somewhere else," these are indeed communications from the source . . . from home.

The energy is ripe with fulfillment. This year is a milestone of energy shift for both you and the planet. It's a renewal of purpose, and a time when you may begin to do things that you have intuitively felt are there for you. But if you consider these communications as part of some circus of entertainment, you have missed the entire reason for the creation of this book. For these communications are each shouting at you that you are just like us . . . eternal and forever, and working in a universe built for you. You are part of the creating force of all things and play a major part in what happens on the planet.

So as you read, consider the voices. They are not *strange forces from beyond,* but rather they are family. The difference between your reality of 3D and ours of multiple D creates a wall or veil that is often difficult to communicate through. But as the energy clears, and as you start to truly understand WHO is speaking, perhaps you might pause a moment and say, *"thank you family, for your love."* Long before you get the 3D message, you will feel us surging through the veil with love for you. You represent a very small group on this planet, ones who would take the time to get in touch with these esoteric things. I know whose eyes are on the page, and I tell you that your lineage is spiritual, and that the time is right for a reconsideration of what this thing called channelling is all about.

Your spiritual organizations encourage you to pray, and you often do. They encourage you to sing songs to God, and you often do. Nowhere in that process do you consider that you are in touch with "entities from beyond." No. Instead, you willingly smile and speak to what you consider to be the creative force of the Universe . . . God. Now I'm telling you that this is no different. When you read these words, it's a two-way prayer, and the force you consider so important (God) is actually speaking to you. Then when you smile and know I'm right, we feel the song coming from your heart. It's time you realized that this is a communication you have asked for and can take part in. It's safe. It's sacred. It's finally becoming common and beautiful, not scary and inappropriate.

So let the family speak to you. Let us fill you with information that will help guide you into the next phase of this great shift we are all within. For what happens on earth, happens everywhere. Difficult to explain, but the truth is that there is purpose for you being here, and what you do has an impact on all. It's time to look in the mirror and not see a single Human who represents one of seven billion. Instead, it's time to look in the mirror and see one energy . . . representative of the life force of God itself.

Let the songs begin!

You are never alone. You are dearly loved.

One

TRANSFORMING OUR BIOLOGY AND SLOWING THE BODY CLOCK

With the phenomenon of science and spirituality being at the forefront, the talk of the town seems to be "talking to our cells." Everybody wants to be able to control their biology at will. Easier said than done.

Instead of "talking" to our cells, don't we need to go about it on an energetic level . . . like visualizing? Isn't DNA interdimensional in nature? If so, how can utilizing third-fourth-dimension communication do the job? Doesn't our biology react to our thoughts instead of listening to our talk?

You are correct to ask the most complex question first. Let's review, for the purpose of this book, the Human Being. It is a 3D creature, living within a 3D environment, eating and sleeping and living a 3D life. When you begin the study of DNA, and especially the esoteric properties, can you really understand it? How can you make the leap to a dimensionality that you cannot even conceive of that's greater than 3D?

Before I even begin the discussion of perception and co-creation, I must ask you this: Are you comfortable with your belief in God? God is interdimensional, and so is the basic premise that you are a piece of God. Do you meditate or pray? If so, how do you cross the bridge from 3D to an interdimensional communication? You see what I'm saying? Some things are "experienced" and understood without any true knowledge of the whole.

Then I ask, can you "feel" the love of God for you? Can you experience the emotions that I might have for you and Humanity when I tell you how much God loves your soul? If you can, you are crossing that bridge, but you are not using your 3D logic to do it. So how are you doing it? This is the key: You are stepping out of your intellectual thinking, that part of you that wishes you to place everything in a box for understanding, and simply enjoying the reality of Spirit that you know is there. In other words, you have learned to suspend your 3D to enjoy something you "feel" is real.

Many people will criticize this very thing! They say that you suspend your logic in order to become esoteric, and in the process you have lost touch with reality. This gives you the brand of those who follow odd beliefs and float around in a cult all day. The truth is this: that all Humanity suspends belief when they want something from God. Even the nonreligious person is willing and ready to receive a miracle of healing when in trouble. There is innate understanding that spiritual things are beyond our understanding. The trouble is when you claim that these spiritual things are yours to work with. This is the "New" in New Age that the old energy has trouble with.

Cellular communication is not hard. It's a bridge already built within your body, ready for you to cross it. The majority of Humanity never does, for you are taught early that your body does what it does automatically, and all you have to do is feed it and all will be taken care of. Therefore, you go about life feeding it and hoping that it lasts. All your intelligence and intellect are based in your head (so you think), and so are all your pains and pleasures. Therefore, you look down at your limbs and organs and hope they work . . . hoping they don't get a disease . . . hoping they don't do something out of your control. If they do, then you say, "I can lose this organ or that organ and still survive." Your brain becomes your entire life, and everything else is expendable to a certain degree, or at least "on its own."

The Universe is like this for you, too. You are aware you are in it, and you know that as long as you feed your body, you can remain in it. Never in a million synapses of your thoughts would you say, "I'm in charge of it." That simply does not occur to you, since you are in 3D and a seeming slave to everything around you.

The truth is that, on both accounts, you are in charge. Universally, you can plug into the seeming chaos and have what you have called "co-creation." This is you, crossing the bridge between your 3D perception and the already existing system of the universe that is all set to "listen" to what you wish to do on your path. Over time, you realize this works, so you begin to nourish the entire idea that you are somehow part of the system and can use it. This is how Lightworkers come about and has been the teachings of Kryon for nineteen years.

Now, apply this thinking to your body. Think of several trillion parts of DNA all identical, organized into the biological system that creates your body system. Do you understand that the DNA is the same throughout the body? Oh, it creates specialized cells that form organs, nerves, and muscle, but the DNA double helix is the same throughout. Start seeing this in yourself as a better understanding of really what is going on.

Let me ask you, Lightworker, which part of you is enlightened? Many will point to their heads at this point. The truth is that the entire system is part of your awareness engine. Your big toe is just as enlightened as your brain. So is your elbow. Do you see? In fact, your very ability to send light is based on using all the DNA at once, creating a quantum field around you that actually is "seen" by the Universe and sends energy into Gaia itself. Picture Humans who are trying to be Lightworkers without knowing this. They try and try and can't feel anything. It's because they have no idea about "talking to their cells" and no idea that the "light engine" needs all of them working together.

The interdimensional attributes of your DNA is more than ten times the size of the 3D chemical double helix you see under the microscope. Scientists even see this, since they recognize that the Human genome only seems to use 3 percent or less of itself to create all the genes in the body. The rest of it is unexplainable. That "rest of it" is the bridge! It's a set of almost three billion chemical parts that organize and structure the 3D part (the 3 percent that is protein encoded). So you can actually "see" the bridge under the microscope in 3D, but since its function is not in 3D, it has no structure or symmetry and is perceived to be useless.

Now comes the good part: Since all the cells are as enlightened as the next one, as you absorb the truth of God, and your own part of the system of God, every cell knows it. After all, they are coming along for the ride, you know? [Kryon humor.] So let's say you have an epiphany of some kind about your spiritual self. You awaken blessed and wiser than you were, and you celebrate your new attitude and knowledge. Now, did you know that your elbow and big toe also "got it"? The only difference is that you never talk to them to know it! All your cells are "hooked together" to participate in everything spiritual. The only thing that is missing is direction "from the boss," and *you* are the boss.

So, therefore, when you begin to address the cells either with your thoughts or your voice or through any possible form of communication, they are already on board with all the facts, just waiting for direction from the person in charge. The real truth is supplied in this paradoxical question: If your DNA is interdimensional by default, why do you think you are a 3D creature? (Now you know the secret.) Your perception is based in 3D, but in actuality the interdimensional engine is already at work within you and will stay invisible until you begin your path of enlightenment. As you study and absorb spiritual truth, you "fill the jar" of your own vibrational energy within each and every DNA strand.

Communication is easy. Don't analyze it! Do you analyze how the internal combustion engine works in your car before you drive away? Do you analyze how a cellular telephone works before you speak in to it? No. You just know it works and you do it! It's time to start driving and calling your body.

One of the great mysteries of biology is how cells communicate with each other. DNA—that is, the blueprint of the body's proteins and amino acids—seems to control every chemical aspect of our being. From the research I've done, each cell undergoes, on average, some hundred thousand chemical reactions per second, and that process, it seems, repeats itself simultaneously across every cell in the body! I'm trying to understand how we can literally slow our body clock, like you mention, within this immensely complex system.

If DNA is in the control room, what is the mechanism enabling individual gene and cell activities to act in unison?

So, on our side, is it the same mechanism that will permit us to work consciously in unison with our DNA?

There is a field structure that is interdimensional around each double helix. This has recently been discovered by your science. [From Lee: Vladimir Poponin found an interdimensional field around DNA that actually patterns light particles in a physics experiment. It was so potent that whatever light the field changed stayed that way even after the DNA field was removed. *http://twm.co.nz/DNAPhantom.htm*]

But there is a communication element that biologists have not yet seen or acknowledged. DNA fields overlap, and therefore they are "seen" interdimensionally as *one field together.* This one field is the quantum element of the Human that is so profoundly affected by your spiritual work and is also the part of you that is spoken to by forces you haven't even discovered yet. So what I'm saying is that your DNA is locked together by overlapping fields that communicate and are "one field" interdimensionally. Here is the secret finally . . . the glue that allows a "whole body experience" that is immediate and ready for healing.

This should again show you how ready the DNA is to "listen to the boss"! For you don't have to logically do anything but "show up" with spiritual intent, and the DNA quantum field is activated within your body. Let it do the work, and you just turn the steering wheel.

From what I know of biology, the hormonal system is the one that pretty much controls the aging process. So to slow down the body clock we have to work directly with this system. For us to be able to change our body clock, as you mention, I think we need to understand precisely how to do it because just talking to it doesn't work, and very few people know what to visualize—the DNA, the cells, the hormonal system, colors. Also, I think we are having a hard time believing we can accomplish such a thing, because mainly we simply don't know how to do it.

Kryon, could we take one example and work with it? Let's take the hormonal system. Would you tell us how we could go about having enough influence on it that it would slow the body clock?

First, do not compartmentalize the body. It's a result of your 3D logic that you wish to address the parts of the engine in order to help this function or that function. It doesn't work that way. Which part of the soup do you bless before you eat it? The salt? The tomato? The answer is that you bless the whole bowl, consisting of millions of molecules of different types.

The spiritual body is a "whole body" interdimensional experience. It does not understand specialized input. It does not understand "I want to age less." Imagine you are a shaman, stepping outside and asking nature to move one cloud to the left for you. Nothing would happen. Instead, nature responds to your intent to move the entire weather system. The ocean responds, the heat and coldness of the water respond, the winds and evaporation comply with the request, and as a result, all the clouds move to the left or are eliminated completely.

Slowing down the body clock is a *whole body experience.* It's part of healing and energy. It's part of voiding your karmic attributes and changing a life's path. We told you early on that there would be those who would see you age less and demand to know how you did it. There you would sit, trying to explain how you take apart soup! Humans wish to separate attributes from the whole and try to manipulate just the items of their choice. It won't work.

Let me give you something you didn't expect . . . a scenario that some will not like: Millions of Humans every day are telling their cells to age less. They are not necessarily Lightworkers, either. They are regular Humans who have no idea that what they are doing is communicating to the cells at a physical level . . . a message that says, *"Slow down!"* They are the ones who are going to the gyms every few days and working out! (I told you that you wouldn't like it.) This quantum field around DNA that I told you about has its antennas out for change and intent. What the Human is doing is telling the cells to change through exercise. It just so happens that this helps to slow down aging. It might seem to be counterintuitive that increasing metabolism also slows the body clock down, but it does. For the body clock is linked to everything around it, including how open your blood vessels are or how able your heart is to pump efficiently. Therefore, many are slowing this clock down without ever knowing it. The body always tries to cooperate with "the boss" (you). When the cells "see" that they are working like they were when they were younger (through exercise), then they begin to slow the aging process to accommodate the change.

Now, add the power of intent of those who can communicate with their cells through a short meditation every day, and you have a real message being given. The cells get "directional intent" from the boss and also proof that they mean it (the exercise).

Anyone who is in touch with their spiritual selves can do this. Spend just a moment each morning as the boss, talking to your cells. Tell them what you wish to accomplish as a whole, not the little stuff. Visualize yourself when you were a child with fresh DNA, before age, before disease, before anything that has happened. Tell them that your intent is for that fresh health. Then if it's appropriate, do some exercise. Anything will help, even a few trips around the block or a few stairs. Do a small ceremony around it . . . thirty seconds . . . so the cells "link" it up to your meditation. This is all it takes.

So . . . does it work for you? If not, perhaps you should examine your "whole body" spiritual experience. Are you really living what you teach? Are you increasing your spiritual understanding, or wallowing in this message trying to find the secret of getting younger? See? It's all related to that connection to the Higher Self, which you cannot separate from biology.

I heard also that we all have a Master cell or Signature cell that resides in the pineal gland; some even call it God cell. Supposedly, this cell contains the entire initial blueprint of our life's journey as a Human, and throughout our life the Signature cell or God cell retains the code of our original perfection and purpose. This cell can be activated by breathing light through the pineal gland, and that energizes the Signature cell that can then bring balance and harmony to all four bodies, from the physical to the spiritual.

Is this for real, or are they talking about the DNA but just in another manner? If it does exist, is it important to be conscious of it and work with it?

The answer is yes, there is indeed a master blueprint. It's metaphoric that it would exist in one place or that it would be in one organ. But it's presented that way for you to work on your pineal gland, which some feel is the "third eye." That creates a smooth pathway for this teaching, for the third eye has always been seen as the ascension structure.

If you have been studying my information regarding what is interdimensional within each DNA double helix, then you already know what's coming. For within the DNA layers is the "Akashic record" layer and also the "God layer." Both of these sound a great deal like the Signature cell, don't they? But they exist in each of the trillions of double helix structures that exist in your body and represent original code and balance between interdimensional worlds.

The "Signature" of your path and your master plan are indeed there, but it's in every cell through DNA, not just one. The idea of this work, however, is to compartmentalize this knowledge into a perception that enables a Human Being to bring the concept into focus in a way that many can easily work with. This method was given to a specific healer for this very purpose, and it has allowed many Humans to heal themselves and "talk" to this master cellular energy.

So, you see, once again there are many paths to understanding the ways of Spirit and many teachings that all lead to the same source, that of helping Humans to heal themselves through profound ideas from pure teachers.

Two

THE DNA OF HEALING

If our DNA contains all that we are, then it has on "file" all of the possibilities of our illnesses but also surely all the possibilities to heal them. But for now, what seems to come out is the illness, not the way that we could heal it.

From what I noticed, when an illness is discovered, then starts the race to try to heal it. Many different modalities are tried—some work; some don't; some also make you worse and can even kill you! I ask because I notice that some modalities work for certain people and not for others. That indicates to me that each person has his or her own signature healing modality, and what could work for some may not work for others.

I know that healing is also a journey, but I think that it could still be a journey even if we knew the right modality that could accelerate the process. Maybe healing ourselves is not very good for business, but it would certainly be worth trying.

Isn't there a test or a way that can also tell us which healing modality fits our energy, our body, and heal us?

If not, how can we do it ourselves? How can we tap into our DNA or our Akashic records to find out about what suits us best? Is it as simple as "listening" to our bodies?

Will we ever see unity between traditional medicine, energy medicine, and alternative medicine?

The test has been around since the beginning. Your "quantum cellular field" (as described earlier) is "body-wise." It knows everything about you and serves as a master diagnostic tool that most Humans have no idea about. You have called it "kinesiology." It's the ability of the body to give you messages about many things: what's happening inside you, what are you allergic to, what is the most beneficial medicine for you, and what message it might actually have for you (such as "Don't eat peanuts" or "There is a disease present").

You are correct about the Human body's specific path. What works for some does not for others. We told you about this early on when we described a time when spiritual healing would be this way, 100 percent for some and 0 percent for others. The only explanation, therefore, is your vibratory rate or, in other words, the measurement of the quantum field around you. The higher it is, the more that this esoteric energy work will be efficient for you. You body knows all, and this test using muscles has always been a key.

Don't you find it interesting that you could have cancer surging through you and not know it? Your body is built to fend off bacteria and many other kinds of disease. It does so every day, and a battle is before it every hour. However, you are not informed about this, since it does so automatically without giving you anxiety about it. If it told you about all this activity, you would be anxious every moment of the day and never get through life. Instead, you are given peace of mind about your biology, and that's all about survival. Meanwhile, that cancer doesn't show itself until you have pain involved, and then sometimes it's too late.

So we say this: How about a checkup every so often using the "body system"? Let it tell you, through asking it questions, about what is happening in your own vessel. Now that I've told you about how the body can speak to you, doesn't it make sense that you can also speak to the body?

The question about today's medicine types some day coming together: The answer is yes. But by then, there will be still another radical healing methodology, so it becomes relative to say they will become one. There will always be something new and unacceptable to those who deal with Human health. But it will work and also be something that is profoundly strange [Kryon humor].

To complete my investigation about DNA, science, and health, I have a last topic to ask about. A new science is emerging that recognizes that living things operate in time to the rhythms of life. It's called chronobiology—the influence of time and certain periodic cycles on biological function. The Human pulse and blood pressure, body temperature, circulation of lymphocytes, hormonal cycles, and other functions of the Human body all appear to ebb and flow according to some basic recurring timetable. These rhythms are not unique to Humans but are present throughout nature. The difference between us and nature is that nature seems to do it instinctively.

I was wondering if we were missing something important in our healing process by not following our biological rhythms or internal clock based, for example, on the geomagnetic activity of the sun.

If we knew more about this science, could the use of medication or treatments be more effective if we followed our own internal clock?

If so, is there a way that we could know this instinctively, like nature does?

Biorhythms have been known for centuries, and even the indigenous used them in coordination to the movement of the tides and the moon. You are indeed a creature of cycles, and what more do you need as proof than to remember that a female's menstrual cycle is coordinated with the moon's cycle? You may also realize that a full moon itself causes disturbance in the psyche of most Humans. So this alone should remind you that you are in tune with the cycles of the Earth itself, and everything on it.

So the answer is yes. A study of the cycles of life on Earth in general, plus the movements of nature, will benefit all of you in your healing process. What this means to you is that there are better and worse times to work with your biology in certain ways. Consider it the "astrology of healing."

Three

RELIGION AS EDUCATION

Kryon, whatever happened the real purpose of religion? Today wars are fought in the name of religion. People are killed in the name of religion. Genocide is permitted because of it. That is without talking about all the sex scandals of recent years. It seems that religion is mainly about a system of beliefs and about who's on top and has the power. Then people have to follow the "top" guy who knows the "truth." Inside that religion, everybody is defending their own beliefs, then they argue about them, and finally, they think it's OK to defend their version of it by eliminating those who don't think like them.

We have some preachers who ask millions from their followers . . . all for God, telling them they will be saved in they share their abundance, when in fact a big part of the millions go directly into their pockets. God is certainly big business for some, a place to hide abuse for others, and for some radicals, an opportunity to make bombs and justify blowing up their own countryman and anybody in the way because they think that they will have twelve virgins waiting for them on the other side!

Maybe I sound judgmental, but from my perspective, religion has lost all credibility. I always wondered where it went. Did we ever have real *religion, the one that teaches purpose, ideas, and putting into practices these ideas—like unity, compassion, leadership, and service? Where did it get out of hand?*

How is religion lived in evolved societies? Did it ever exist in a civilization like in Atlantis or Lemuria?

There was never a religion in Lemuria. Instead, there was intuitive understanding that life was all about nature and that Humans could control their own future. This was the core of spirituality . . . an intuitive knowledge that each Human is responsible for all the good and bad things that happen to him or her. Lemurians also had two interdimensional DNA layers of activation at the quantum level, allowing them to be able to "see and understand" things that are still invisible to you. So this helped them with their relationship to God.

When these layers started to fade, Humans turned to the spiritual structures you see now . . . a combination of mythology and history, often wrapped around a prophet that they were fond of. The rest, as you say, is what you have discussed.

However, do not be too harsh on organized religion. The search for God in any Human life is personal. His own truth is what he perceives and accepts, even if it's part of a doctrine around things that never happened! What I'm saying is that all Humans are blessed by searching for God in whatever ways they wish. Within their search, God is indeed there and will respond. So there is no judgment around any organization that tries to find God in its own way with integrity.

Like so many things, however, religion has been abused and managed with power and inappropriateness. So has almost everything else! So again, it's up to each Human within his or her scope of discernment, about what is, and is not, real spirituality. It's easy to stay on course, however. The rule is this: *Stay with ideas that are balanced in love.* Watch out for those who tell you that God is in a box of their own making or that there is only "one way" to become enlightened. Run the other way when you are given a list of "rules of God." For these are the attributes of men in power, not the attributes of the love of God. God is not a controlling force. God is a releasing force. Look for the love.

Religion is here to stay, but the integrity of it is beginning to be an issue. Finally, after all these years, followers may just start asking enough questions that they force the upper echelons of the church to "clean their bell towers" and start presenting the love of God in a fresh new way that actually blesses the masses instead of themselves. Look for a more empowering message coming from all of them in the future.

Four

MY PERSONAL EXPERIENCES

All of us are experiencing many changes and challenges along our spiritual path that can also lead to some powerful experiences. We all live this process in different way. None is better, only different. The purpose of inserting these personal experiences in the book is that I think many people can relate to having experiences themselves but not having any clear explanation for it. It is simply to show how spirit works.

About twenty years ago, I was at a New Age event in Toronto, Canada, with my brother. At a distance, I see two persons creating quite a fuss. At the beginning they were pretty far, so I couldn't see what the fuss was about. Then I decided to get closer, and as I approached, I saw children circling them, laughing and being very excited. As I looked at them, I realized that something special was happening but didn't understand what. But I was astonished to see that they where dressed in silver one-piece suits! They were going from one table to the other talking with people, so I went back to mine, hoping that they would stop also at our table. As they arrived at our table, I noticed their physical features. I never, to this day, saw more beautiful persons (or beings). They seemed perfect in every way—their bodies, their hair, the color of their skin a perfect tone between white and black; they had spectacular green eyes. It was a feminine and masculine energy, but for some reason they seemed to be each other's version. I still remember them quite clearly. They were so calm with all the fuss around them, because at that point, there were a lot of people around them.

On our table, we had books and a picture of Master Hilarion. They said hello and looked at our things and picked up the picture and said, "We know him very well!" Then they left. I immediately told my brother, "I think they are drop-ins." I never forgot that experience. Kryon, you said once, "Don't be surprised if some day the ETs who visit you get out of their crafts and look just like you! This is a reference to the Pleadians, who are part of your seed biology. There is no scheduled arrival for them, but the potential exists that you may indeed meet them."

Were they ETs? Were they Pleadians, like I think they were?

Do they often do these kind of visits? What was memorable is that the children seemed to instinctively know who they were and celebrated the event.

Yes, dear one, you saw it correctly. Celebrate that the Pleadians care enough about your enlightenment that they are here to keep watch. They come and they go, and often they attract children. They are only watchers and are keeping track of their "garden." For they know all too well that the Human Being is a brother, whose DNA is Pleadian.

Do not work this up in any way to a fearful thing, for they are loving partners with you in this experience. Do not make them anything but what they are: loving observers of what they helped to begin in all spiritual appropriateness. For they are your "seed biology."

THE SECOND EXPERIENCE: PERMISSION
TO GO FORWARD . . . OR MY PERCEPTION OF IT

At the end of 1990, I was pregnant and living pretty happily with the father of my child in a beautiful house in the country. One day, I was having a gathering, and one of the guests was a channel. So just, for fun, I asked him, "Is it a boy or a girl?" He said, "For now, it's a boy!" I said to him, "For now? How can that be?" And he said, "Yes, sometimes, it changes." Frankly, I didn't really believe him because I always thought that I would have a boy. Then one day I went to the hospital for an examination, and the nurse examined me and said that everything was fine. She asked me if I wanted to know if it's a boy or a girl. I said fine, knowing very well that she was going to say that it was a boy . . . and then she said, "Congratulations, it's a girl!"

Fast-forward, two and a half years later. . . .

It is 1993, and I'm now living alone in a small apartment with possibly no job, no money ahead of me, in debt, and with a child to support. One night I am in my bed wondering what is going to happen to us . . . talk about being at zero point. That night I am awakened at 4 A.M. with a very vivid dream, with the feeling that it was very important that I remember this particular dream. Basically, the dream was about a friend of mine having a baby, and her husband presented me with huge tray full of cakes and sweets. After looking up this dream in a book, it said, "The birth of the baby meant a new beginning, a new life is upon you, and the tray of sweets meant you will reap the sweet rewards of life." I knew that it was a message from above telling me to hang on. This had a huge effect on me. I never doubted after that dream that I would be fine. In 1994, I began my mission as a publisher of spiritual books.

My perception of this event is that a sort of question was asked at a certain point on an unconscious level about what I chose to do. In my opinion, it had to do with the Harmonic Convergence and all that followed. I think that possibly some people had the neutral implant before it was even known.

Kryon, if my perception is right, was this experience about completely changing my path and giving permission for implementation of enlightenment (neutral implant)? Without even asking for it, is it possible that I received it without knowledge that it existed? If so, why do some people receive it before knowing about it? Could you explain how this is planned?

You are correct about what we originally called the "neutral implant." It is the implantation of permission to change spiritually, something that can void your karma and change everything in your life. Therefore, many had asked for this years before anyone every heard of Kryon.

The Harmonic Convergence only created a better energy for it to work, but before that it was also very doable. Many Lightworkers before the 1987 event did this, and many had already accomplished this shift, without having a name for it or doing it consciously. But within the new energy, it is now something that is far more common. So after the Harmonic Convergence, we spoke a great deal about it and how to do it.

Meanwhile, it has been available for a very long time. After all, don't you realize that the past masters of your history all did it?

The change of sex in your child was also of your own making. One perception of it being a boy was a predisposition you were going to experience due to your old path. When you had a change of path, the gender changed, since you needed another energy to work with. But, contrary to what you think, nothing happened inside the womb, however! This is a paradox of time for you in 3D. You might say, "If I had not changed my path, I would still have had a female child! It was there for nine months!" The truth is far more complex. Spirit saw that with free choice, you were going to change. So it was not predestined, but, rather, the potential was there so strong that it became reality. Therefore, even before your path change, the gender was set up to be a female. All this, while you were convinced it was a male due to your perception and to those who "read" you in an old potential energy.

If this confuses you, think of it this way. Spirit looks at potentials. Every decision and potential life change you will have are represented. Although the answers are unknown as to which way you might go, the potentials of what may happen "glow" a little brighter than the potentials you may not do. This is because of the energy you are in at the time of the prediction. It's a situation much like a tarot reading, where only the energy of the moment is taken into consideration, as you do a "future spread." It seems like a paradox, but in our time it is not.

Here's another example: A woman is going to get a psychic reading. She is carrying a female child due to *her future decisions that Spirit knew she would make.* These are strong spiritual potential decisions from the synchronicity she was about to create. She comes into the room with the words "It's a boy" written across her forehead. The psychic "reads" what's on her forehead, since the reader is still looking at the older energy before the pregnant woman made the decision to change.

My partner (Lee) came into the world with one kidney and predisposed seasickness. He tried to get into the Navy and never made it. [From Lee: They turned me down fast!] His predispositions were created due to the strong potential that he would do the spiritual work he is now doing. If he had gone into the Navy, there was a strong potential that he would have ended up in Vietnam on what was called a swift boat. Although we have never said this before, the other potential on that life track was that he would not have returned. Do you see? Before he ever made a decision to work with Kryon, his body was being prepared due to the potentials we see. His birth attributes kept him away from his old karmic desire to get into the service, thereby saving his life for what he is doing now.

Notice that in both cases, the strong potentials were realized. Lee indeed began to work with Kryon later in life, and you also make the choices that you did, now bringing these words alive to thousands of readers. Having a female child instead of a male was very necessary for you to move into the energy you did, and so it only looked like a switch in 3D.

We don't expect you to understand this paradox of time, but we will always try to make you comfortable with the fact that your free choice, and potential free choice, is the key to your immediate co-creation. Also, can you see the love in this? God cares about all of you.

THE THIRD EXPERIENCE:
TWO POTENTIAL CRASHINGS?

About two years ago, I was in my car with my mother and daughter. Arriving at some traffic lights, I start to slow down a bit, but then I see that my light is green so I accelerate. As I am accelerating, I cannot see the other car coming in the other direction because of some trees, but since I have the green light, I suppose that any other car coming will stop at their red light. As I'm about to cross the road, I see that the other car is not stopping—and that is when I have this bizarre experience. I see myself having the accident. I see the man's face looking at me, surprised, not realizing that he passed through a red light without stopping. I even hear the noise of the metal when I crash into his car, but then, I hear the brakes and see the car just pass really fast in front of me. When it's finished, I'm in the middle of the street, and I know that something happened. My mother and I look at each other wondering how we avoided such an accident.

Did I imagine this, or did two potentials cross paths? If so, what decides that it should happen or not? Was it a karmic residual?

You did not imagine this! We have spoken many times about how your predisposed karmic path is voided when you begin to control your own destiny. When you do this, you may still live in the same town or even be driving the same car you might have had on an older track. But these "near misses" all represent something that might have happened if you had not gotten off the predisposed path. So your intuition is correct, and you saw an old plan pass before your eyes.

We have told you in many channels the following: *Blessed are the Humans who realize they do not have to follow their karmic predisposition, for they will often pass by their very own deaths on their way to a long and happy life.*

When you take charge of your destiny instead of simply going down the groove that was given to you, you change yourself, your life's direction, and your time of death.

Five

MOVING CLOSER TO 2012

THE POLITICS AHEAD

For many countries, the years to come will bring many changes in their government. We see now that many countries seem to be electing more and more female head of states. But what seems to be emerging at the same time is that the "old guard" or the old energy doesn't want to let go. There is a saying that goes "Dictators never leave power." This seems to apply at the moment. We just have to look at Putin (in Russia) or Chavez (in Venezuela) or Magabe (in Zimbabwe), who make every effort to put laws into effect so that they can stay in power. These are only three examples.

At the United Nations I mentioned this . . . that the last gasp of old energy would be seen as those in power trying everything they can to remain. I also mentioned that the new energy would slowly dissolve the chest-pounding macho leadership that the Earth has seen forever. It is turning far more feminine (gentle), and the public will begin to elect those who represent this. Take a look at something astronomic that is going to happen in 2012: another Venus Transit. Ask your astrologers the significance of that transit, and you'll know even more about this [Kryon humor].

In the dictator nations, coups will eventually happen to replace inappropriate leaders, and the potential of one of them is right upon you.

LIVING THE GREAT SHIFT

From all the information that I have gathered through the years, this shift is a very atypical one. The planet surely feels like it is shifting and shaking on all sides—and we are, too! Probably because it is shifting with us on board. You said recently in a channeling that I listened to, "Your body is ready." Well, frankly, Kryon, for many of us, our bodies seem to be falling apart rather than feeling that we are ready. We all have different physical symptoms—headaches, fever, loss of focus, depression, and all kinds of sleep disorders like inexplicably waking at every hour in the night, and so forth. I know that it is all part of the package, but it is sometimes difficult to make the difference between physical problems and spiritual symptoms. To say the least, it is pretty intense.

So I'm asking, Kryon, from your perspective, how is our body ready? Are spiritual symptoms going to continue until 2012, or are they going to be less and less intense?

For some (me included), a lot of the symptoms seem to be above the shoulder, with the eyes, ears, and jaw. Is this a specific pattern for some?

Remember that you were born in an older energy. Now you wish to take your New Age body, which is floating in the Old Soup, and make it all wonderful. Well, it won't be for a while. Almost all of you are currently suffering the attributes of the shift. As the energy of Gaia starts to move to a higher vibration, your body is reacting. It can't stay in the old, and it can't move to the new. So while the shift is happening, it hurts!

We told you that a major shift happened in this very fashion between the last months of 2007 into the new year of 2008. There was an actual withdrawal of spiritual attributes for a time, then a replacement with new tools. This is the shift we told you about in 2000. Now, here you all are, and it's beginning to happen.

Spiritual symptoms are often in the head. Yes. Also ringing in the ears is part of all of it, since you indeed mention ears. Skeletal structure issues also are prevalent, with the feeling that there are problems with the bones. This is all about energy, however (even though you are convinced it's about getting older). It will be with you past 2012. So engage energies that will help you with this growth process. There are many, both esoteric and chemical, that will help. Watch for new chemistry from the jungles.

Six

FOLLOWING THE NUMEROLOGICAL PATH OF THE GREAT SHIFT

For the benefit of my readers and because of the importance of the year 2009, I would like to give them a numerological path until 2012. I think this would help to put into energetic perspective what every year holds for possibilities of change and transformation until 2012, to better prepare us to "ride" the last years.

I would like to start with 2007 and go until 2012—just enough for them to understand the numerological value and the energy of these years.

2007 (9): THE YEAR OF COMPLETION

Beside being a completion year, I noticed that communication seemed to be "frozen," especially in the last months of the year. Nothing happened. Were we at a place that I call "the corridor," where we closed a door and not quite opened another one? Was that another "zero point" in our lives?

Look for combinations of 9 against 1, as in 2007–2008 and again in 2016–2017. This, of course, will happen in eight years, another 8 for you to look at. But let's talk about the one just past.

Even if you sit in the last part of 2008, there was something remarkable about this transition that is worth mentioning today. The 2007–2008 transition was the first time this particular transition math has happened in this, the first millennium of the 2000s. It is the first occurrence after the millennium shift. Add this up and it represents a nine (9) and a one (1) together. Indeed, this combination happens every decade, but this is the first occurrence. It is the first one within the generation of the 2012 transition! All of this should have been flagged for you. You should have looked at it very carefully and said, "What might happen when you're going from 2007, which is a *nine* (9), to 2008, which is a *one* (1)?" Nine represents "completion," and one represents "new beginnings." Wouldn't you think it means something? Now look at the numerological meaning of the number representing the distance between this "completion" year, 2007, and 2012. The distance between 2007 and 2012 is five years. You say, "And what does a five (5) mean, Kryon?" Five is change! What is the numerological value of 2012? It's also five (5). Just think: change/change. Tell me, if you believe in energy, do you think this sequence of events is trying to tell you something? Dear ones, I have just given you a scenario of what I wanted you to read because of what you went through in 2007 and especially during the last four months, heading into 2008.

I'm going to explain something to you now that is very difficult for my partner to relate to, for it is not linear. 2007 was an end year—completion—the very number shouts "the end." Let me tell you what it is really: *It's a reconfiguration of an energy platform that will allow you to go into a new beginning platform, fresh and clean.* It is not an upgrade. It does not take an old energy and add to it. That is linear. You expect linear change; you expect all things to happen in a linear fashion. If you exercise a muscle, over time you expect it to get bigger and bigger. The more you exercise it, the bigger it will get. And you apply that same logic to energy in general. But that's not the way it works from Spirit.

The energy that we give to you is interdimensional and spiritual in nature. It is not linear. There is an attribute that took place in 2007, something you need to know about because in the last four months of that year, the energy you depended on, the energy you thought would always be there, the things that should have happened in clarity, did not! Seemingly a collapse began instead of an advance to better things. Many of you had life challenges. Some of you lost connection to spirit altogether! Some of you began wondering where this is going and what has happened, and why you didn't get what you were working toward. So I'll tell you: *All that took place is a winding down of all the gifts and the tools you have come to depend on, in order to bring them to zero. Then they reconfigured and burst upon the scene with renewed and more powerful potential. They came back in the middle of the month of January 2008.*

So there was a space of time from September 2007 until mid-January 2008 that you had to work through. This reconfiguration is not linear. It doesn't make sense to you why the energy would have to go away just so it could come back! But that is the way of it in a reality you don't experience on Earth. Some of you went through challenging times in the last part of 2007. I know who reads these words. Oh, dear Human Being, do not blame yourself for what has transpired or what has not transpired. Don't blame yourself! For it is common with Human Beings and reflects a

3D "cause-and-effect" relationship. It's common for Humans to blame themselves profusely when things don't go the way they think they should, spiritually. You are used to being responsible. But at that period, you were not!

Now I give you two examples of this, and they may shock you. You didn't expect that I would talk about these people in this lesson—precious people—a man and a woman—two thousand years apart.

Consider for a moment the Jew called Jesus. He's on the cross, being crucified and seemingly at the point of death. Recorded history will say—and not accurately, by the way—that he cried out, "My God, why have You forsaken me?" He didn't say that, actually. What he said is "Where have You gone?" Jesus the master felt a withdrawal. He felt all of the guides, all of the entities that he counted on, were gone. All of the wisdom drained from his body. He felt the darkness and the blackness invade him. It went through the bubble of security that he had counted on all of his life, as the Master of Wisdom and Love that he was, and he cried out for help. It was noted, transcribed, and given to you. It's history.

Now, did you ever ask yourself how someone so close to God could have had such an experience? Just when he needed his entourage the most, they left! Let me tell you this: What he experienced was a nonlinear shift of energy. He was taken to zero for just a moment . . . just a moment, so he could go into something called ascension. Then it all came back. Unrecorded was what happened after that. You didn't know what happened next. You didn't hear him go "ahhh." It wasn't recorded, you see? The love of God poured into him, with more power than he ever had

47

before. That's the way it works, and for a moment he blamed himself as the Human he was. For just a moment . . . for a moment . . . just a moment, he questioned his faith.

Let me tell you about a precious woman whose whole life was lived under the umbrella of compassion. The older she became, the more compassionate she became. And she is one of you [in your modern times], and her name was Mother Teresa. I would like to tell you about this woman. Did you know she died in sorrow? You might ask, "Why would such a woman, who was so close to God, die in sorrow? With all the things that she had been doing, with the reverence that had been placed upon her very name, allowing for sainthood itself, why would she die in sorrow?" It's because she was a linear Human Being who did not understand the shift of energy upon her.

Years before her death, along her path, her energy shifted. She had earned it, and it went to zero for a moment. The old station she used to tune to was gone, and a new frequency was there, begging her to change the way she did things so she could find it and be joyful, with more power and compassion than ever. But she didn't understand. She thought that she had been left alone—lost her connection.

Why would God do such a thing? Why would God depart from a saint of compassion? And I'll tell you the truth: God never did! What happened was that she misinterpreted the change of energy. It's the same thing that is happening in a general way right now. It's going away slightly, so it can come back strong with new attributes. And this compassionate, beautiful woman did not understand that she was being asked to tune to the next station, literally change the way that she meditated, the way she contacted Spirit. She would have to go around the protocol she had been trained in and speak to the master directly. But she stayed with her teaching, and nothing happened. Her training in an older energy kept her in a prison of protocol, and then she died in sorrow. Oh, but she never lost her compassion, for that was her gift right to the end.

Don't blame yourself for what transpired in the last months of 2007, for they were trying times. The advice during an "energy shift" is *Do not change your path. Don't make any startling moves because of what's happened or what you feel at the time.* These are times that are difficult especially for Lightworkers. You seemingly think that you have lost your connection for a while. Continue through, knowing that the energy will start to change again. Some of you have felt this more than others. Some of you have stayed centered so that very little was felt. Others have been devastated! You have not understood what happened; now you know. I know who is reading this. Don't blame yourself!

Now let's talk about the Good News. 2008 has brought you a new tool set. Those who know how to co-create will find this to be far easier than it ever was before. Some of the things that you have been waiting for, the messages that you have been waiting for, the abundance of the synchronicity you have been waiting for, is there for you to finally realize. This message is timeless on how Spirit works with these kinds of stair steps of energy within important times. This is especially true in the first part of a millennium shift, especially as you are heading toward 2012. New co-creative gifts are upon you.

Co-creation requires synchronicity. Synchronicity requires that you stand up and go and be and do, in order to meet those who'll create the synchronicity with you and for you. God is not going to fall on you with a miracle as you sit there praying.

2008 (1): THE YEAR OF NEW BEGINNINGS

What seems different about this year is that it is a completely new level of energy. From my understanding of your channeling, you talked about the idea that it was not simply "putting a new spin on an old energy." It is a transfiguration platform for us to go to a new platform.

THE NEW ENERGY

My partner stood on a stage in Israel many years ago, where I gave him information for those who spoke Hebrew and Arabic in the room. Many had cried out and asked, "When will things change?" I gave my partner the information that he was to state on stage for all to hear: Not until 2008 would Israel and Humanity in general start to see a shift. Finally, some of you will understand this and why it was spoken so many years ago. The potential was always here. The transition from nine to one was always there. We foretold this and gave hints of the potentials along the way; and some of you caught it, and some of you did not. Now, here you sit in the middle of it. There are new tools. There are enhancements, and the beauty of this message is that it is not just for Lightworkers. The Earth is shifting, if you've noticed.

UNDERSTANDING THE CHAOS

Number 1: Many of you are now going to start to make sense of what formerly was chaos. That is to say, the very way that Spirit works with Humans on this Earth, which has seemed chaotic, which has seemed accidental, is now going to start to make sense. It will make sense in a way that will make you more comfortable as you count on the answers coming as you need them. It is truly a shift of dimensional thinking. You will begin to have an understanding in your mind in a way you cannot justify in 3D of what is taking place. What this means to you is that you're going to be a lot more comfortable in your skin. Even those of you who call yourselves Lightworkers, those of you who call yourselves metaphysical, will start to see the planning. You will start to see the potentials and will start to see how chaos isn't chaos.

That's a gift, for up to this point, it has been very tough in a three-dimensional state for you to make any sense at all out of the answers that were coming your way. Blessed are the Humans who have sat through this learning all of these years and have had such faith! My partner has given you a phrase: "3D shouts and faith whispers." And what he means by that is that your reality, that which you expect, that which you were taught, that which is everything you are, *shouts* at you. But the ways of Spirit, the seeming chaos in that interdimensional space of nonunderstanding, whisper. And so what happens is 3D always wins. It drowns out the little voice of the whispering that says, "Listen to the love of God." So what we're telling you is this, dear ones, that the shouting of the 3D is going to start being reduced. The concepts are going to become more equal, and you're not going to have quite as much trouble in the transition. That's number 1.

SELF-ESTEEM FOR LIGHTWORKERS

Number 2 is something you probably didn't expect and something you probably didn't even know. I will give you an axiom. The ones with the lowest self-esteem on this planet are the Lightworkers. Did you know that? And the ones with the lowest are often the healers! Perhaps you wouldn't expect that, since these are the ones who are in touch with Spirit. These are the ones who have the gifts. But they often sit in an energy that does not support them, and when Human Beings sit constantly in an energy that is uncomfortable, they are uncomfortable. The 3D-ness of their personality is affected, and self-esteem is part of that.

As we have said before, we know who you are. You may carry your head up high, but we also know what you do when you're alone. We know what you think when you're alone. We've heard your cries: "Why me? Is this ever going to be solved? Will my family ever understand? Will my partner ever understand?" I'm going to tell you something that's going to happen in the new energy, for it is finally shifting. It's going to be the great equalizer. It's slow, dear ones. It's not going to happen overnight, but this is the beginning of it. This is much of what you've been waiting for, Lightworker. The self-esteem of the Lightworker is going to start to come up to the magnificence of what it represents. That's because they're not going to be in an energy anymore that is against them. It's going to be an energy that supports them.

Slowly, many of you will begin to feel it, where Gaia and you are aligned for the same purpose, the potential of peace on Earth. Look for this everywhere, and the first to feel it will be the Lightworkers and healers. I challenge you to celebrate. I challenge you to build a statue somewhere for the energy that is shifting that you are done with! Now, that's going to be counter-intuitive to everything Humans do, for they only build statues when something bad happens. Maybe it's time to shift that consciousness. Why don't you make a memorial to what you have accomplished in some way and celebrate it? At least blow up a balloon somewhere! [Laughter] Oh, Lightworker, do you understand what I'm saying? You've come of age. 2008 was a *one*, and that is a new beginning. You're going to start receiving the support you've always wanted and worked for.

SEEING THE BIGGER PICTURE

Number 3: You're going to start seeing the bigger picture, and it's about time. Picture this: The attributes of learning and spiritual path walking in the old energy had you clueless and in the dark. Until you reached that place where you needed help, nothing happened. That's the place at which you were delivered the solution. That is the map that is talked about in that fable called "The Journey Home," channeled for my partner many years ago. Expect that "map" to change. The bigger picture has you seeing beyond the problem. The bigger picture puts you in a situation that is more nonlinear; that is, you are less constricted by the time line from past to future. You will be more comfortable seeing *into the now,* for the now is an energy that does not honor or respect linearity of time. The solutions that are going to come to you in the future are going to be more expected. They're going to make more sense to you than what you have seen in the past, because you are seeing a bigger picture. These concepts of which I give you now are advanced, and some of you do not understand them and may very well wish to listen or read this again. If I had to summarize it, I'd say that Lightworkers are going to be more comfortable with themselves and their relationship to time.

ALTERNATE HEALING BECOMES
MORE MAINSTREAM

Number 4: Healer, stand back, because the things that you have are about to be enhanced. Oh, it may take a while, but I will tell you that the things that are the most spooky to those who do not believe in what you're doing will become more mainstream. Expect science to be developed behind energy work. Expect those to come to you from places you didn't expect, because what you have works! When this starts to happen, you can say, "Yes, I see it happening!" And when you do . . . blow up a balloon, please! [Laughter] Celebrate it. Oh, dear ones, I'm telling you that when you celebrate, you acknowledge to Spirit that these things are happening. It's like you are acknowledging the things you didn't expect but knew were there. That's becoming interdimensional. Faith becomes reality, and healing will be easier.

What I'm saying is that these things are going to be easier. Why? Because the energy of the age is upon you. Because the magnetic grid has been postured since 2002 for this very thing and now it is yours. "Oh, Kryon, when will these things begin to happen?" I'm saying they're beginning now, but you won't see all of these things all at once. You're going to see them as you work them. Let it be known that no Human Being can sit back on his heels and wait for the miracles of God to fall in his lap. The part of the issue here is that the Lightworker is going to be asked to get up and push on the doors. Find the synchronicity that works the system, and claim the new energy that is upon you.

CONNECTION TO THE HIGHER SELF

Number 5: It's going to be easier to connect to the Higher Self. Isn't it about time? There are many celebrating angels right now, and they're singing a magnificent song. I wish you could hear it. The choir is amazing, and there is nothing like the interdimensional voices, notes that cannot be heard by the Human ear, light that corresponds with them in frequencies too high to be measured, and sound so high it melds into the colors of light itself. And if you could hear the songs they're singing! Listen. Listen to the lyrics! Oh, your name is there, and it's your angelic name, the one you have that is forever and is not your Human one. What they are celebrating is that you have brought this about, dear Human Being, an age that was not predicted, an age that no prophet told you would occur, and there's so much evidence that you're sitting in it.

I say again, where is that Armageddon you expected? I say again, where's the doom and gloom that all said was going to be upon you? I say again, where is all of that negativity? Oh, there'll be challenges—there always are. I will enumerate some of them for you in a moment, but you've lifted yourself out of an old energy that you've been in for thousands of years, and you put upon this Earth an energy that no one expected. And the light that you have created has been done so by less than one-half of 1 percent of the Human race. That's how powerful it is. If you're listening to this message and you have no idea what is taking place, let me tell you this: This is not an elitist message. It's not just for the esoteric people. There's no judgment of you, and I know who you are, too. You are as loved as any family member. Why don't you look at this? See if it's for you. You don't have to, because it's free choice, but there has been a beautiful thing happening on this planet, and that's what I'm talking about today.

THE RELATIONSHIP TO GOD

Number 6: You're going to feel much, much more comfortable in your Lightworker skin than you've ever felt before. A relationship with Spirit is going to seem brotherly, sisterly. It's no longer going to be God and Human Being if you want it to change. This is going to require that some of you are going to channel. Are you ready? Oh, not out loud perhaps. As I've said before, it could be channeling of your Higher Self, just for you. Don't be afraid of this. The words my partner uses are a channeling of "you with you." Don't be afraid of the love of God in your life. Don't be afraid of transition in your life. Everyone sees change as so frightening, but what if it's a solution to your problems? Is that OK with you? Think of massive positive change.

THE CHALLENGES OF THIS NEW BEGINNING

Now let me bring you an itemization of some of the things that will come with the others, which are perhaps challenging in their own ways and different, even a proclamation of a new energy attribute that will change my partner's life.

TOO MUCH LIGHT

The light that you have you cannot contain anymore, and this will start to be seen. Just when you thought it was safe! [Laughter] As long as you held that edge, right? You can't hold it anymore. Human Beings will know what you're into, and they'll know what you're doing. Remember, we told you of this day. We told you of the battles between the light and the dark; we told you that there would be those who would not accept what you have. Watch for this, for there will be more around you who will not accept what you have, and it just comes with the territory.

You can't have spiritual power and the light that changes lives without it being noticed. No matter how silent or humble you are, you are filled with Spirit and the love of God, and people will notice. And you will be forced to explain it a little more than you are now. "Well, Kryon, what am I going to do? What will I say? Do I tell them I'm a Lightworker?" No. Why don't you tell them you've fallen in love with God? Why don't you tell them that you've seen yourself in a different way and you're comfortable in your skin. Why don't you tell them it's not threatening to their lives or their churches, and it's just *you with you.* Let them see God in you and not be frightened.

FEAR OF THE LIGHTWORKER

The second one is related. Many will be frightened anyway. Light does that. On an Earth that has been postured in a dark energy for thousands of years, which suddenly has light in it that it never had before, many will be afraid. If you are used to the dark and suddenly there is a light, you cover your eyes and wonder what it could be. There will be those who wallow in the dark, who enjoy all of the dramas of their life, who are victims and enjoy being victims, who will run from you . . . run from you!

You represent something they don't understand, and the irony is that what you carry could heal their lives, stop their drama, and lift them up. But they won't touch you. They're afraid of being burned with what you have. Powerful, you are! Watch for this attribute, and even if you expect it, you won't understand it. You will say, "Why is it that they don't like me? Why is it that suddenly there's such resentment or betrayal? I'm only carrying light!" It's fear. Fear of the light and what it represents in a dark world. Will it affect you? Of course.

So expect it, and know what to do. You'll be prepared. When it happens, just love them. You can't heal the world, dear one, if it doesn't want to be healed. All you can do is let your light shine. The ones who see it have free choice just like you do. They can accept it or run away. Do not be judgmental toward those who are not ready for your discovery, for they are as loved by God as you are, and they have their own paths to discern as they walk this planet in lesson.

MESSAGE FOR LEE CARROLL

Third is a message for my partner [Lee], given for all of you to read, so that it is known. For this is important, and if I just told him, he might not tell a soul and keep it to himself. This way, it is public.

For years, I have given him the admonition about media. For years, I have told him it is inappropriate to channel in mass media, especially what you call broadcast. This is in reference to linear broadcast that is not requested, which flies through the air and that you pick up if you randomly choose a station or frequency that you "pop onto it." Suddenly, here you find Kryon speaking.

It's inappropriate and it still is inappropriate, and he does not have permission to put any full, recorded channeling on the air. Oh, there may come a time, but not now. However, he now has permission, from this point on, to do *two things* that he has never done before. One: It is now permissible to put designed samples of channeling on the air, which he creates. Snippets, if you would say. Sound bites, if you would say. Two: He has permission also for the first time to go into channel one-on-one and have interviews with Kryon, answering questions from the interviewer. And he's not going to like that, since he is not evangelic. It's part of the new energy, my partner. It is part of a general public becoming ready for acceptance or rejection. And there will be many who see him as the clown. Yet I will tell you, it is the love of God that has postured him for this, and it's the love of God that will get him through it.

FAKING IT

It's going to be a whole lot harder to fake this process called channeling, because there's going to be a lot more people and Human Beings of both genders who are going to see the lights. They're going to know if it's real or if it's not real. Many will be revealed as doing it inappropriately without any sacred energy, only themselves. Get ready, for those who do it inappropriately to gain power or control or notoriety will be seen clearly by both sides, Lightworkers and non-Lightworkers.

Look for the integrity of the love of God in every single word. Look for the integrity of the love of God, which will always shout its love for Humanity, shout those things that are noncompetitive, shout acceptance for every single Human Being who listens, without judgment. That's the God who you know. That's the One who you're in love with. That's the One who washes your feet today.

The energy of Spirit is not compartmentalized or structured into a doctrine. There would be those who might hear this and say, "It's got to be the devil." And there are those who will hear this and say, "This is the love of God." It is the consciousness between the two that represents the free choice of a Human Being. It represents closed minds and hearts; it represents fear of change.

I would like to tell you that this entity called Kryon is in love with Humanity and would never bring you a message that is inappropriate or filled with doom, only one that magnifies the magnificence of who is here in the room and those who listen and read, called Humanity. Don't look at this and say it's inappropriate because it doesn't follow some earthly doctrine that you have developed from the mythology of the ages. You can't do that. Do your homework. Feel the love that is here. Then decide for yourself outside of the boxes that you were taught within. Let your heart make the decision.

Watch for those who would wish to take this to a controlling level. Now, my partner, you know why I have given you permission to speak on the media with me: to help combat those who will try to fake what you have practiced for nineteen years.

THE SHIFT IS UPON YOU

The final one is this. Prepare for shift. It has been coming, and you've had the channelings that said so. It is the Great Shift, and it begins. It is the beginning of the preparation for what the Mayans told you would happen as the Earth shifts into the year 2012. This magic year, which many fear, is only the signpost that comes by in your time line that says you are moving into a new energy that was foretold by the angels. There will be no significant spiritual happening in 2012, only the celebration of the signpost that tells you that you have arrived.

It's going to be different. For those of you who don't like change, it's going to be fearful. So prepare for it. All these things I bring you are positive, filled with light, even within change.

Begin preparation for something we told you long ago is potentially possible, even in your lifetime. This is what you never expected, and that is the slow development of peace on Earth. Watch for a changing Middle East. Oh, it won't happen immediately. But the seeds are there. I speak now to those ears that are Hebrew and Arabic, and I'm telling you this: Your time is starting to come. It's what you've asked for and what you've prayed for. There is beginning, a consciousness of compromise in a difficult land. It is upon you. Watch for it; pray for it; send light for it; be part of it, for it is yours to claim.

Don't pay attention to your news. They are going to bring you the worst of the worst. They always do and always will. It is the way of their system. Your media will look for the worst thing that is possible, the most abhorrent thing that has happened on the planet that day, and they will zero in and they spend all of their resources on it. They won't tell you about the other things that are going on. Right now in the Middle East, they won't tell you about those who are trying to build peace outside the government. They won't tell you that there are hundreds of thousands of them on both sides of the issue who are coming together right now. Your news has never reported that. It's just a little too hopeful. [Laughter]

2009 (2 AND 11)

For me 2009 is a turning point, and 2009 seems to carry two numbers, 2 and 11. So we pass from number 1 to number 2 but also number 1 to number 11, an illumination energy.

I was wondering, is it a double numerological year?

Is the year 2009 the year that Humanity gives another permission to change, a go-ahead for the last stretch?

There is going to be a hundred years of the number 2 alone, so the 2 is not that special in the dates, although it is the number of duality—the struggle between light and dark. So the year 2009 truly is all about 11, not 2.

Eleven (11): You can look at 11 in many ways. First, it is two 1's together. They clearly indicate new beginnings, twice. When you see any number twice, it is a powerful indication of what each one means. Back in 1987, the Harmonic Convergence later acquired a numerical nickname, established in 1992. It was 11:11, and you have been seeing it on the clocks for almost a generation. This is what I mean. For 11:11 is a double 11 and therefore is like saying it twice for emphasis.

Next, the 11 is a master number by itself and should never be seen as a 2. Eleven means illumination, or the result of the establishment of light. It is a transitional year toward 2012, coming out of 2008, which is strongly about new beginnings. The 2009 transitional year truly is one that is about "light preparation." My partner tells me that in your terms it means "Get your house in order" (because of the next year, 2010).

2010 (3)

Following an 11 year, what will be the energy of the year 2010?

This is not a pleasant number for some, for the 3 is the catalyst. A catalyst year is one that lays there ready for something to happen that would propel the Earth into major change. The "3" years often become the years of war. Don't read anything into this, for these years are often the years of resolution and peace also.

In your case, there is something lurking here that may sound like a prediction, but I don't make those. [Kryon smiles.] I can tell you that there are several potentials regarding Israel that glow very strongly during this year. Do not fear any of these things, for they represent the effort to create a lasting peace in the Middle East. There are many who do not wish this and instead wish to wallow in fear, despair, and uncertainty. It feeds their lifestyle and creates power within their own lives and internal social structure. Terrorism is about the survival of a very old club, representing an energy of the way things used to be solved.

At some point in time this must be resolved, and often the resolutions for those who want violence create even more violence for them. This is the way of it, that those who wish to create chaos on this planet will pull it to themselves. So do not mourn for those who decide to live by the sword, for it is their free choice to die young in this manner.

2011 (4)

I think you said that number 4 represents Gaia.

The number 4 is indeed an earth number. It represents two strong attributes: The first is that it is the number of Gaia. The other is that it represents structure (there are two structure numbers, 4 and 8). This is normally a number of peace and represents a time of reflection and closeness to the planet.

The potentials for this year, however, are dramatic. For it sits next to the "third rail" in metaphysics, which is the 2012 energy. (See next answer.) It will be a year of reflection and preparation for Lightworkers. Much fear can be generated during this year from those who do not understand what the Mayans were really working on. For the Mayans were a culture who studied the esoterics of the movement of the bodies in the sky. They were not entirely about solstices and eclipses. They were about the long cycles of vibration on the planet. Their information was that 2012 marks a transit to the "yellow sun" energy or, in their verbiage, a shift into a much higher vibration than we have ever seen. [From Lee: The glyphs on the temple walls in Xochicalco, Mexico, clearly show this!]

2012 (5)

The year of change . . . what is the indication of that year.

Do not place too much energy upon this year. Indeed, it represents change, and that doesn't sit well with many people. But more than that, it represents the "signpost" as you drive past it on your ever-moving 3D time track. It simply says, "Entering 2012—the year of the beginning of change for planet Earth."

The year 2012 has a potential of solution. By then Humanity may have actually moved faster than the potentials, or slower. So these things are never the way they appear at the conception of the information that is being given. Therefore, what I'm telling you now may happen sooner or later, but at the moment, you are on target for this year being very special.

Celebrate this year, and give the Mayans credit for esoteric prophesy, not low-energy savagery. For their civilization lasted a very long time, and there was much variety over that time. Do you wish to be known in history for your worst city's poor crime rate? Or do you wish to be remembered for your grandness and clear environmental vision? You see? Celebrate the Mayans for the alert that they gave you about a very important time, a time when your vibration is ready to meet the energy of 2012.

In closing, dear ones, we are in awe that Humanity has passed the marker and is headed for a new energy. We understand that for you it is slow going and that these things seem to take a very long time to evolve. But for us this is not a waiting time. It is a time of action and preparation. For what you are seeing every moment of every day is an evolving Humanity. On this side of the veil there are many coming right back in a very fast turnaround, ready to create what many said could never happen: peace on your planet.

The most significant thing we do is to represent a creative force to you that is becoming closer and closer to being understood. It is finally within the grasp of the regular Human Being to have what many have called mastery. This represents the ability to hold an energy that can change the immediate life that is looking at it. There is a reality shift at hand where the Esoteric Human Being will no longer be the outcast or the one who believes in odd things and joins cults. For you are beginning to close in on the very real ability to change your own future, heal your bodies, and become a logical addition to spiritual belief on the planet.

Science is starting to agree with you! The best science on the planet is beginning to prove many of the concepts of the esoteric belief system. It's obvious why, since true esoteric belief depends on intuitive communication with an innate source that you have built into your cellular structure. Science is beginning to actually give credit for this force, for it drives Humanity to absolute truth and represents more than fifty thousand years of Human experience built right into the DNA. Science is beginning to give more and more credit to intuitive thought, seeing that it is the instinct of the Human Race, and it has been implanted there through the ages, ready to be seen as a viable spiritual truth. It trumps mythology and Human religious organization, and begins to shout that God is not what you thought. God is bigger than you thought and is part of a grand and loving system of support for all of Humankind. And the Human Being is in the center of this system.

Kryon does not give prophesy, since your future is your own and is the product of what you decide. But Kryon can see the potential strong points, or the most probable outcome of the energy of the year 2009. This energy speaks of Gaia becoming a much stronger partner with the Human Being. To you, this means that the process of living as a Lightworker will become an easier life. It means that the energy of Gaia will become far closer to what you are trying to do on Earth than it is now. Many of you are aware that since you entered into your esoteric beliefs, the energy around you was thick with unbelief. The structured spiritual belief systems of your culture denied your ability to be accurate or even to exist. You didn't have the credentials or the history or the validation of the giant spiritual corporations of the Earth to do what you are doing. So they have discarded you.

What is possible now is that your credentials will begin to be developed by the reality of what is happening to the planet. This reality is already positioning the mythology of your spiritual doctrines in a difficult place, since what has happened is not in their prophesy. In fact, it is the opposite of their prophesy.

The Armageddon did not happen, and instead the Soviet Union fell over, never to reappear. Your event of 9/11 took place, which was a huge energy event that had never been prophesied by any spiritual leader in any belief system anywhere. The peoples of Israel and Palestine are trying to put together a one-state solution, right in the middle of some of the greatest old energy tensions that have ever existed in Lebanon.

Your science has declared that "intelligent design" is the way the Universe was created and that it could not have been an accident. Biologists are declaring that there is something in the DNA that makes you search for the creator and have called it the "God gene." Do you see? These things are staples of the New Age! They shout that perhaps the old doctrines of organized religion are based on old history and do not represent what is actually happening. The result? Don't expect an exodus from the church. Instead, expect the church to begin to bend their positions on what the love of God is really about—compassion and life change, instead of victimization and protocol.

The best advice we have is what we have always had. It never changes: Do not fear what is happening on the planet. Do not fear the integration of God into your own life. Do not fear the love of God. For it may feel different to you to take on a more responsible role in your own life, but you have an enormous entourage of angelic beings that are holding your hands. This is the truth—that you are changing the vibration of the Earth.

And so it is . . . .

Part Two

MARY MAGDALEN AND THE HATHORS

REGARDING WHAT MAGDALEN HAD TO SAY: AN INTRODUCTION TO THE MAGDALEN SECTION FROM JUDI SION

I'm going to be bold in what I write to you because I think the time for boldness is upon us, especially upon us women.

I find it ironic that all too frequently, when we get an e-mail or a letter about *The Magdalen Manuscript,* it begins, "Dear Tom" as if I, Judi, weren't a participant, though they often go on to write about the section of the book that I wrote, which is Every Woman's Story, in truth. My ego doesn't mind the exclusion, but my heart minds that the female is so easily dismissed, and I can't help but wonder why almost everyone addresses the male before considering the female. The whole subject of the book is about a return to balance and specifically the return of the feminine, yet people who write to praise the book (and we have genuinely never received any negative letters) never even consider the feminine presence involved in the creation of the book. If we cannot consider the feminine presence in creation, what hope is there?

Why do I bring this up if my ego isn't involved? To point out the obvious: that the feminine continues to be not only overlooked but also almost ignored in what is considered the modern world. (I would argue we have not evolved much in two thousand years. We have only the *appearance* of evolution.)

I love the material Magdalen gave for this book. It is a clarion call to the women not to be silent. Silence kills. It can kill through the horrible simplicity of a woman keeping her mouth shut for years, only to get cancer, invariably of a feminine part of herself. Tired of being quiet, and stuffing it, her body will cry out for attention, one way or the other.

Are you really going to be silent while the entire world is taken over and leans so far to the right that we fall into a fascist abyss, with evangelical governments and evangelical religions of all persuasions in control of your every movement? A zealot is a zealot, whatever god they bow down before.

We stuff it. We take care of the men, and we stuff it. I have listened to every single word Magdalen has said since we first contacted her at my behest, in 2000, and I'll tell you what I think I've been hearing. The men aren't going to do it for us. They are not going to stand up and make the difference that is required. Magdalen has voiced, on several occasions, her sadness at how easily and quickly women turn on each other, in our proclivity for jealousy and manipulation. We must put that aside. We must stand up and be counted, and we must speak our truth—no matter what.

The greatest lesson I have ever learned is to not care what anyone thinks and to speak my truth. And I have learned this principally in my sacred relationship with Tom because I had to get to a point where I didn't care what even he thought, despite my love for him. I had to get to a place where what mattered above all else was what *I* thought—my truth. And if speaking that truth cost me this relationship, it was a price I was gladly willing to pay. This is not selfishness, and don't be fooled by religion into confusing taking care of yourself and taking back your power, with selfishness. Taking care of yourself and taking back your power are the road to mastery.

I hear Magdalen calling for the women who read her message to be heard. I hear her asking each of us to speak our truth. What do we fear losing? Do we fear losing life? Then we don't really believe life exists beyond this plane of existence. If we *knew*, really knew, that life continued beyond this, what would we fear? Losing consciousness? If consciousness continues beyond this plane, what do we have to fear? Do we fear losing our loved ones around us? Why do they matter that much to us that we would fear their disapproval over our own truth?

My old teacher used to say, "Reason it out, Master." He called us Masters. He used to say we would never comprehend that we are good, divine beings, as long as we call beings outside ourselves master and do not call ourselves master. He also used to say, "Look around you. There is no one around you who would step in front of a bullet to save your life. If they wouldn't die for you, why are you living for them?"

The question haunts. Who are you living for?

We are being manipulated by our governments and by our religions into a dark place of fear. Fear consumes the brain with tentacles that reach over it and surround it, cutting out the light of reason, keeping you from thinking. *You cannot teach a fearful, worried mind.* You can reason out everything that is happening around us and see how information is being twisted to keep us subservient and fearful. Look within for your truth and speak it.

I have found Mary Magdalen to be the most eloquent and masterful of all the channeled material I have worked with, and I have been editing channeled material since 1986. And Tom and I both are deeply committed to her words being printed exactly as she says them, verbatim. After all, her voice has been quieted, and she has been lied about and used to demean women and our passion for over two thousand years. She says the time of that ignorance and imbalance is coming to an end. So be it.

FROM MARY MAGDALEN

I have a deep fondness for, and sweet memories of, my times in France. It was here, after all, that the bosom of St. Maries de la Mer received me and my child, Sar'h. We were harbored here in safety. And when I headed north, into what is now England, to protect Sar'h with the Druids, I remembered France. And when Sar'h grew to be a woman, and I gave her to be wedded, I was free to return to France, and I did so many times, teaching the mysteries as I understood them, and the traces of my travels still remain there to this day.

When I returned to England for my final days, France was deeply in my heart. The knowledge of the feminine mysteries, if used in the manner in which I hope they shall be used, will impart a healing balm upon your Earth.

The rise of the feminine in this time does not mean the disenfranchisement of the male. Women must be raised to equality, and then in the depths of the Human psyche, the sun and the moon shall be balanced, and the great universal androgyne will emerge. And from this mystery of the joining a spiritual renaissance will come forth. That is my prayer for you individually, that you may be raised up through a spiritual renaissance within, and I wish it for your Human family. May the lies, the sorrows, and the tears of the past be wiped away.

So be it.

Seven

THE ORDER OF MAGDALEN

You mentioned in your book The Magdalen Manuscript *that you were part of the Magdalen Order and that it was hidden. Why was it hidden? Does this order still remain today?*

The term *Mary of Magdala* refers to the region from which I came. You see, Magdala was an area, geographically. So that was my title. It was a convention of the language, to refer to someone in that way, as in "Jesus of Nazareth." As Yeshua's work continued, a circle of women formed around me. These were women of power. These were, in a very real sense, Yeshua's disciples as well, but they were not in the inner circle. They recognized my spiritual authority and that I was the holder of the inner teachings of Yeshua. We did not have a name then. We were in secret. When I left for France, to save my life and that of my child, they remained. At that point they called themselves the Order of Magdala and continued for some time, giving that which I had given them to other women, in secret.

This was not a *formal* order in my lifetime, not like there are formal orders of nuns now. It was more of an informal gathering of women of power who followed Yeshua and me. The number was thirteen, including myself. I was considered the head of this group, which was loosely called the Order of Magdala.

Were they present at the Last Supper?

They were not present at the Last Supper. I was the communica-
tor of the mysteries to them. Occasionally Yeshua and I would
meet with them, but mostly I was the center point around which
these women gathered. They were woman of financial means and
social power. We met in secrecy, by necessity.

We remained hidden simply because that is how it was done
then and, I might say, how it is still done today. Men would
hold the positions of prominent power, and women would place
themselves behind the scenes. It is a way of doing things that
still exists to this day. So the cloaking of the identity of the
order—which was an informal gathering of women—was a
cultural convention.

Whenever a significant undertaking is begun, if it is to be
sustained, it must have support. That is what this gathering of
women was about, the support of Yeshua's ministry and also the
cultivation of his teachings through myself.

Those who associated with me were chosen by me because
they were evolved enough to understand what I needed them to
do. They understood the work needed their assistance and their
allegiance, and so this "coven" (which simply means a group
that meets regularly in secrecy) formed out of necessity, because
one cannot create in a vacuum. You need allegiances; you need
a group. We did not identify ourselves as the Magdalen Order
during my life, but we understood we had formed because of my
connections.

Later, after I was far gone from this world, women of power
looking for a constellation point around which to gather, formed
various groups, the Order of Magdala, the Order of Blue Rose,
based upon their conception about what our work was about.

If there was any formal order in my time, it was out of the Temple of Isis.

There is no specific organization that has continued since that time under my direction. There are some who claim they are continuing an order that I began and that they are responding to direction from me, and all I can say to that is this: *My teachings have a resonance, a field of knowledge, that can be accessed, and people of power, spiritual power, can access this information and bring it forward, and I actually honor this, but in terms of any formal order receiving direct instructions from me . . . it is not so.*

Eight

TEMPLE OF ISIS

When I say that the only formal order to which I belonged was the Temple of Isis, I am referring to my training and the mission that I undertook when I entered into the Mysteries of Isis.

I began my training in the Isis mysteries when I was twelve, under the tutelage of my mother. Since my mother was Egyptian, it was her intent to pass on to me this knowledge she possessed, and she began it when I turned twelve and entered puberty. When I was eighteen, I entered the temples in Egypt for the direct training from the priestesses, and this was the final marking point for my mother. She had done what she intended to do.

In many ways, I was an odd duck, as you say. I was a Jew, and I was, at the same time, trained and initiated into the mysteries of the Egyptian goddess Isis. This may seem odd to some, but think of it this way. In your era, if you are from an educated and moneyed family, you might be a particular religious persuasion, but you might have studied and been educated in areas of the world different from your native land. My family was highly educated and quite wealthy, and in the ancient world it was quite common for those with means to visit the cultural worlds of power, and these included Greece and Egypt, and other areas in the Mediterranean as well. My family had roots in Egypt, which is why I was sent there as part of my education.

When I was in Egypt receiving this formal training, I was initiated into the Temple of Isis, and I formed a direct relationship with Isis within the understanding of that time. I found it of interest that Isis had some similarities to what I had learned earlier about the Shekinah, the Judaic feminine aspect.

Shekinah is an expression of the primal feminine power of transformation. She cuts through obstacles and impediments. She shakes things up, and she extends the feminine balance—although it is a fiery aspect, not a gentle, soft presence. The Shekinah is raw, fiery, and full of trembling power. She was never a physical being, but she exists energetically, just like Isis exists energetically.

So you see I was, at a personal level, attempting, you might say, to bring into balance the cultural understanding that I had been given, which included the Shekinah, the transformation feminine energy, and what I had learned of Isis through the temples and through direct contact.

My direct contact of Isis occurred in what you would call meditation. We were trained to enter into windows of the mind—you would call them altered states—and through these windows of the mind we could have direct access to Isis or other deities as well. In some regards, this was not dissimilar to what you now call channeling in that I would receive information from Isis, but I did not speak it or communicate to others. The only exception is that when tested I would report to the priestesses what I got through direct contact, and if they had gotten the same thing, I would pass. If it didn't match what they got, I would fail. This is the only time I shared what I received.

I, a young Jewish girl, heading to Egypt for education, was recognized by my family and by my teachers as being of "high quality." I was recognized as being of a high caliber, but no one knew that the finger of Isis would be placed upon me, so to speak. So I went to Egypt simply to expand my mind, to gain an understanding about another culture, and in the process I became aligned with Isis.

REGARDING EMANATIONS AND INCARNATIONS

Isis herself never fully incarnated. She was far too smart to do that, but she did incarnate emanations of herself.

Isis is a transcendent energetic expression of the feminine. She has a body, but it is in an energetic form; it is not physical. She can be experienced directly in her various forms—and she has more than one—in what the Egyptians call the Duwat (the spirit world). But she herself does not have a physical form.

When one encounters her in the Duwat, she can have a Human form, the form of a woman, and this form of a woman sometimes has wings. So the forms that a goddess or god takes in this other world, the Duwat, can shift, can take many aspects, and can be seen in different ways depending on which aspect is being expressed.

So at times one will encounter Isis as a loving, nurturing goddess, and at other times she may have wings, and one may fly with her into the heights of spiritual awareness. If you have angered her, she may turn into a column of fire. So there are many forms available to Isis, all of them depending on her state or mood, you might say.

She exists at a very high level of vibration, meaning her world vibrates very quickly. It is a realm of light. As you descend into matter, the vibration rate decreases, and things move much slower here in the physical than they do in the realms of light. It is simply physics.

When Isis, in her compassion or understanding, determines that her presence is required here in the realms of matter, she can cause an emanation, a light fragment of herself, to incarnate into a Human form. But she never fully incarnates. For instance, when Isis incarnated in Mary, the mother of Yeshua, it was a very powerful presence, yet it was still only an emanation of Isis, so that Mary, the Mother, was a mixture of both Isis and herself.

Isis would never descend from the realms of light into the realms of matter and Human form. She is far too wise to undertake such a thing. So an individual who might have a fragment of emanation of Isis would possibly have deep feelings and connections to Isis herself. But I would say to such a person that it is important to realize that it is an *emanation of Isis* and not Isis herself.

This possession of an emanation is a treasured thing, but it also creates quandaries, because if one imagines one's self to be Isis incarnate, then one is deluded, because, in fact, it is only as aspect, a small part of Isis that resides in one's being. So the task for such a person is to live his or her life as a Human—and, paradoxically, an emanation of Isis can show up in a male body (to make things more interesting).

So it can be confusing for one who possesses an emanation of a divine aspect, and it can be confusing for those around such a person. And here is why. In one moment the *divinic* energy can be expressing itself through the emanation, and there can be a clarity and a spiritual power that is unmistakable, and those around such a person in resonance to this emanation will be deeply moved and touched.

In the next moment, however, it can shift from the emanation to the Human, and suddenly where there was brilliance, there is dullness; where there was compassion, there can be hostility; where there was impeccability, there is now manipulation, and everything in between. And so a person around an individual who possesses an emanation can be very confused. This confusion arises from their belief that the individual *is* the god or goddess incarnate and can do nothing or say nothing that is incorrect, when, in fact, the individual is a mix of energies.

It can be confusing for the individual possessing the emanation if he or she does not understand or recognize the thresholds between a pure emanation and the distorted Humanness—the vagaries of the individual's Human personality, in other words.

If the people around such a person do not recognize or understand this, then they might give their power away, believing that everything the individual says is divine. This would be an error and potentially dangerous.

So I consider it a vital necessity that those who possess emanations of a divine attribute recognize their territory, so they know when they have stepped out of the emanation and that they have the spiritual impeccability to let those around them know. But, unfortunately, such is not always the case, so it is the responsibility of those around such a person to take this into account and not take everything that is said as coming from the "mouth of the divine" but to discriminate and recognize when the emanation is speaking and when the Human is speaking.

And let me say this. We live in a very vast universe, and I have not encountered all beings, but based on my experience, I have never seen or witnessed a full embodiment of a divinity. Always it is an emanation that has incarnated, and it is the responsibility, and the necessity, of those who encounter beings who possesses such emanations to be aware of this. And the reason this is so is because oftentimes the person possessing the emanation identifies with the emanation and is not aware of other attributes in its personality. I feel this is vital information, especially now in this time, because many divinities are sending emanations into this world.

So I would like to reiterate something I just said: *I have never seen a divinity fully incarnate.* I would imagine that some readers immediately recognize the intellectual implications of that statement, but for those who don't, let me fill in the blank. The statement applies to all beings I have encountered, including my beloved Yeshua.

He possessed a clear, powerful emanation of the divine. When this emanation spoke, worlds trembled, and yet as one who lived with him, he had other aspects as well. In other words, Yeshua was a mix of God and man. He had his moments of doubt, uncertainty, and personal suffering. There are those who would like to believe that he was always a clear beacon of light, unwavering, unhesitant, and always self-assured; and while this was his usual state, there were times when he was uncertain and caught up in his own quagmire. As a woman in love with him and as his confidant, I found these moments when he shared with me his personal darkness to be treasured moments.

And always he was able to transform himself back into the pure light of his emanation. For that act I was in awe and am still. For me that was one of his greatest miracles—that he could return, ever faithful to his own divine emanation. That is the essence of spiritual mastery that I witnessed in him.

RETURN OF ISIS

When I refer to the return of Isis, I am talking about two aspects of her return. One involves emanations of her into this world embodied in individuals. And in a more metaphorical way, as a return of the honoring of the feminine and the expression of the enlightened feminine qualities in this world—and this takes place through individuals. So what you are finding now in this world at this time and the coming years is that more children will incarnate with divine emanations. This is already happening.

There is already a seeding of Humanity through children who possess divine emanations, Isis being one of these (divine beings sending emanations). As these individuals affect those around them, it will be like a cascade into Humanity of enlightened attributes. Parents of enlightened children will find it most interesting and challenging. What you are witnessing at this time is the seeding of Humanity with divine emanations in the form of individual young people.

In some cases, older individuals (meaning not children) are suddenly awakening to the fact that they have an emanation of the divine within them.

I want to be clear here. All beings possess divine emanations, you might say—but I am not speaking about the divinity of each Human being. I am speaking about literally an incarnation of an

84

aspect of a divinity into the body of an individual person. This is qualitatively different. Such individuals are brighter and possess powers of consciousness that others do not. The effect of such individuals living in this world will not be fully seen for about twenty years.

The other aspect of the return of Isis that I refer to is metaphorical. This is simply a shifting of cultural imperatives, and by this I mean that the days of patriarchal domination are ending. This domination is ending out of necessity, for in spite of the density and seeming stupidity of the collective Humanity, there is a shifting of awareness, and we will see this very much more clearly in the coming years.

There shall be a recognition that we *have* to change—meaning Humanity must change how it lives in relationship to the Earth—Earth, as the Great Mother, the Great Feminine—and this will spread out, if you will, into all expressions of the feminine.

One other aspect of this metaphorical return of Isis is that more women, especially the younger generations of women, will be taking the reins of power—not asking permission—they will simply take the reins. And the growing number of men, especially in the younger generations, will gladly share, for they will know with unyielding certainty that it shall take two—male and female—to bring Human civilization through the portal of these times.

Nine

DA VINCI AND *THE LAST SUPPER*

One of the greatest works of art in history is The Last Supper *by Da Vinci. From my research, Da Vinci seems to be part of a group of people called the Literati. It was a great knowledgeable force of people that included men and women. He seems to be a great supporter of the divine feminine energy. It is obvious that when we see this painting, there is no doubt that a female presence is sitting at the table to the right of Master Jesus, and today, we all know that it was you. At that time (and maybe even today) the person sitting at the right of the most respected person meant that this person was the second-most respected person.*

Cameras did not exist at that time, nor was it possible to take snapshots. This painting was a moment in history and Da Vinci did his rendition of it.

In my opinion, for him to do so, two things could have happened. One of these is that he knew how to access the Akashic records. He was such a genius for his time that when we look at all his work, we know that something extraordinary took place for him to be able to do so. The other option is that he was there at the time, and he simply could remember this event.

Would it be possible to explain how Da Vinci had the inspiration to do this painting? Was this Last Supper a preparation of Jesus' disciples to continue his work? Since you were present at this gathering, what was the purpose of this reunion?

What is the holy grail about?

Yes, I was present at what is called the Last Supper. And I did sit on Yeshua's right side, for I was, in his mind, the disciple with the highest attainment, and I was the one who received the innermost teachings.

Da Vinci painted this painting (*The Last Supper*) from the Akashic records, for he certainly had a highly developed mind and spirit. He was part of a tradition of a loosely bound lineage of artists and thinkers who understood the place of the feminine, who cultivated the hidden knowledge when it was dangerous to proclaim it openly—for the dark veil of the church had obscured the divine feminine in all forms. And so those who shared this knowledge did so in a cloaked manner, intimating the presence of the feminine but never showing it clearly. This knowledge of the feminine, the place of the goddess, came from the pagan roots before the church dominated civilization.

The cup that was used at the actual gathering called the Last Supper was, ironically, a very humble clay cup. It was not ornate in any manner, very unlike the embellishments of artists of later times. It came to be believed that the cup, the Holy Grail, had magical properties. This is, unfortunately, a Human tendency—to believe that a power resides somewhere *outside* and that such a power can be possessed.

The true Grail cup is the womb of the feminine. And in this instance, it was my womb, for I had conceived Yeshua's child. And so it is ironic and tragic that men have pursued the sacred Holy Grail when all the time it was around them in the women of their lives. This is a time when this error can come to an end, when the Grail cup can be recognized for what she is, and woman can be elevated back to a place of balance, not domination.

It is my observation and expectation that this change will be instigated not by men but by women, specifically women who have the courage to speak their truth, to rock the boat of culture and society. These are the heroines of the hour. And the world is sorely in need of them at this time.

What is now called the Last Supper was an odd moment for me personally.

I knew that the situation was moving toward some type of climax. But the intention of the gathering was to transmit spiritual power. So when Yeshua broke the bread into the pieces, as he handed it to each person, he handed not only the bread but a type of spiritual power. It was a transmission, and the evening was electric. So it was primarily a means to transmit power. He knew he was going to face the death initiation.

Ten

MISUNDERSTOOD TEACHINGS

I would say, as one who has received the inner teachings of Yeshua, that a great misunderstanding has ensued regarding his teachings. The essential point he was trying to convey was that all persons possess divine power. It is a gift given to all Humans, but it is something that has to be cultivated. If it is not treasured and protected, the weeds of ignorance, the gnarled roots of Human negativity, will overtake it. And so he was constantly speaking about the need to tend the garden of one's soul.

He used metaphors in teaching because I believe he was a poet at heart and understood that the metaphors were like doors that opened to the soul. So when he said you have faith the size of the mustard seed, he was saying it only took a little bit of faith. But he was not a believer in blind faith. He believed in the type of faith that produced results.

He saw that in the Human heart there was the possibility for the seeds of love to blossom and change the world, and he believed this love was from the father and the mother, for even in his prayer you call the Lord's Prayer he began in Aramaic to call upon both mother and father, but this was lost in the translation.

It was a prayer to both the Great Father and Mother, but the place of entrance was through the inner self. He believed that the living divinity was within the *self*, so when you pray to mother/father, it was to the father and mother inside you, and from there it went to the large aspect. So it looks like praying to something outside yourself, but in reality it was praying to an innermost aspect of self, but an aspect that transcends the personality.

Yeshua was the heir to a long-standing understanding and tradition of the balance between male and female, so when he prayed it was to both father and mother. It was not his creation to conceive of a trinity that left out the feminine. This was not his creation but the creation of individuals at a later time, individuals who manipulated his teachings for their own end. Now, in this time, these things that are in error can be corrected, the truth brought to light, and the lies of the last 2000 years brought to an end. So be it.

Why was the balance of the feminine and masculine "shut off"?

There are many ways of looking at the abduction of the divine bride—the eclipsing of the divine feminine by the patriarchy.

Certainly the great matriarchal cultures that extended through the Mediterranean and into Europe and Africa were deeply affected by the fall of Rome. In the ensuing chaos, it was an act of political desperation to unify the many diverse and conflicting religions. It is certainly an unfortunate footnote to history that when Constantine attempted to solve the problem, he did so with a gathering solely of men. But this tells us how deeply the exclusion of the feminine had occurred, even at the advent of the Council of Nicaea. From this moment on, the misappropriation of the feminine within what was presented as Yeshua's teachings escalated.

The tragedy of this, from my view, is that what was handed down as the teachings of Christ were so far removed from his actual understanding, and for the next two thousand years his teachings were used as a cloak for terrestrial power and dominance and manipulation. Now as we turn into a new cycle of time, that misunderstanding can be corrected, and the distortions of the Human spirit can be healed.

Why would such a period of two thousand years be necessary? Why did the mother principal need to be obscured? Why did the feminine in all her expressions need to be so demeaned? I do not have a precise answer. Perhaps it is one of the cycles of time. But I am heartened by the realization that this cycle of patriarchal dominance and suppression of the feminine is about to turn. The divine feminine is resurrecting through the hearts and minds of women and men who are evolved enough and courageous enough, and their numbers are increasing.

And so I look at the distortion of the last two thousand years and the misappropriation of my beloved's teachings as dust that is to be swept from the living temple of the Human spirit, and let no man or woman stand between you and your own divine nature. So be it.

Eleven

THE RETURN OF THE DIVINE FEMININE—THE DIVINE YOU

It is my belief and my expectation that the divine feminine will show up in the hearts and mind and actions of women.

It is not that *she*—the great cosmic mother—will descend from the heavens but, rather, that she shall express herself through the life choices that women are making now and will make in the coming years.

This return of the feminine will not express herself solely through women, but also through the actions of men. For men are as much victims of the imbalance as are women, although certainly on the surface of things they hold the reins of power. But by only holding one side of the rein, the masculine side, and by refusing to share the other rein with the feminine, men have damaged themselves. And so the return of the divine feminine will show up in the hearts and minds of men as well. For they shall realize—those who are evolved enough to realize—that they cannot continue to live the way they have and that the Great Earth, the Great Mother upon which they live, has been harmed. And so part of the return of the divine feminine is a change of attitude toward the Earth, for indeed the Earth is a feminine aspect as held in the collective psyche of Humanity.

How it possible to explain that the reemergence of the divine feminine is not about "the women taking over the planet"? I think, in a very profound way, this is the fear of many men.

At an unconscious level many men in power are reluctant and fearful of the rise of the feminine. At a very fundamental level it has to do with survival. For men who have held superior positions of power and economics, allowing women to have the same status and income as they have is perceived as threatening. Perhaps at a deep subconscious level some men fear the rise of feminine power because they project onto the feminine the sword-wielding Medusa who will smite them with her anger, and while this may be a form of the feminine some women do, in fact, express, it is not the overriding expression of the divine feminine.

The divine feminine yearns to be in balance with her divine counterpart. The desire for relationship is deeply embedded in her nature, so men really have nothing to fear about the rise of women in balance. In fact, I suspect they will find it quite freeing to no longer be shouldering the delusion that they are responsible solely for the world, a concept that is truly delusional.

Another more deep aspect of this is something I alluded to in *The Magdalen Manuscript,* when I said that one of the most difficult passages for the man was to separate from his mother, because there is such dependency on his mother in the early years of his life. This subservience is imprinted in his psyche. Each man must find his own way of transcending this. Each man must find his own way to disconnect the women of his life from the mother of his childhood—and so it is a very complex affair, this rising of the female in balance to the male. It affects all levels of your culture and psychology. I would say to men who wonder about what it means to have a feminine in balance to the masculine: It means a new type of freedom and end to the delusion of isolation, an end to the necessity for martyrdom, and the birth of a new kind of world, a world that will be worth living in.

Twelve

PRAYER, GOD, AND INTENTIONAL CREATION

The great mother/father god is an impersonal power—a creative potency that operates independently of Human consciousness. It is the ever-evolving process of cosmic creation. And this takes place due to a fundamental creative tension between what can be called the male polarity of consciousness and the female polarity of consciousness. It is involved in the creation, sustaining, and destruction of all cosmic forms. It is not aware of, or particularly interested in, individual Human beings. It is not a consciousness that one would "pray to" in that it is not a person. It is the process of creation itself.

This process of creation extends from the great cosmos down to the individual creatures of Earth, including man—all the way down into what you now call the atoms and subatomic particles that make up your body.

This is mother/father god, embodied as you.

Yeshua understood that one could be in communion with this aspect of mother/father god. But let's, for the sake of argument, leave the word *god/God* behind, and let's, for now, call it "creative potency." This creative potency exists within you in a very intimate way. It is the very source of your breath. It is the very source of the beating of your heart. It is the very reason you can understand my words. For this creative potency exists in every level of your body, from the most minute atom, to the molecules that make up your form, to organs, and even your mind, your mental experience of the world. All of this, all that you are, is an expression, one expression of this creative potency. Your brothers and sisters, your fellow Humans, are also unique expressions of this same fundamental creative potency. Thus, metaphorically, you have/you share the same mother and father. All the creatures of the world, the animals, the plants, they are all unique expressions of the same fundamental force that has expressed you. What Humans possess, as a divine gift, is the capacity to be aware of this creative potency, this living divine power that *is* you.

So when Yeshua said "mother/father god," he was speaking poetically about this creative potency. And he understood because he had been trained in the ancient knowledge that all creation proceeds from a union of opposites. For Yeshua, this creative potency was not an impersonal power. He knew that one could form a relationship with it in the inner sanctum of one's own soul. For he, indeed, understood that here, in the inner sanctum of one's being, the creative potency was very personal. So through this inner door, Yeshua entered into union with the creative potency, and it responded to his intentions, which he called prayers. So I would say for those who, in this modern time, are disturbed by the misinheritance given by the church and who find the word *prayer* distasteful, and the word *mother/father* god disturbing, substitute *creative intentionality* for the word *prayer* and *creative potency* for *mother/father god.*

Yeshua's point was that one does not need to go to the temples to pray—indeed, that it was useless—that the connection to creative potency was within. So this made him very unpopular with the priesthood, both of his time and with the priesthood of the Catholic Church. So they (the church) incorporated the master teacher and made him the hallmark of their power, but a very fundamental aspect of his teaching was that you don't need to go to the temple or church—because he/she won't hear you—because where you are heard is in the most inner part. *When you speak with intention, things move. You can move the world.*

What would you understand as being a "sacred relationship"?

Sacred relationship is essentially the establishment of a relationship upon the solid bedrock of truth. It is very unusual in this world, for lies and manipulation are left behind in this form of relationship. The two persons involved meet on a common ground of authenticity and reveal the naked truth to each other and to themselves—both the truth of their glorious nature and their defiled negative attributes. Then, through the fire of transformation, the dross of their defilements can be transformed into greater awareness and spiritual power; and then this increased awareness and spiritual power is turned back on themselves again for never-ending refinement of dross into gold, ignorance into enlightenment. It requires courage, impeccability, endurance, and a very good sense of humor. It is not an easy path, but it is the fastest one home to the Great Self that one is.

Is it possible to attain this? It depends on the individuals involved. Whether one is in a sexual relationship or not is immaterial. If you wish to test the waters to see if this path might be for you, enter into a relationship with a peer, your equal. Make the vow of truth to each other, and then live through the terrible consequences of this—terrible because it is frightening and terrible because it is also uplifting. It is the path of the spiritual warrior.

If you could give a message to every woman at this time, what would it be?

I would say this to each woman: Find the courage to speak your truth. *The return of the goddess is through each woman's heart and mind. Through the act of speaking your truth, the world will change.*

I say to each woman, find the courage to open the door. Don't leave it locked! The door I speak of is the door of the heart, for the woman holds in her heart a fierce truth. But only when it is shared or spoken can the world change. *This is the touch of the goddess.* Women have been trained to remain silent, to ask for permission.

In this time, those women who find the courage (must) give themselves permission in speaking the truth that lies within the heart, whether it be joyful or full of sadness, content or full of anger.

This truth must be expressed. It must be spoken. And it must be listened to if this world is to change and if this world is to survive. There are levels upon levels in this.

The Earth—as Cosmic Mother embodied—has been speaking through her loss, through the species that are disappearing. This is her truth.

And so there is a parallel between the Earth and all women. It may be that you, as an individual, cannot speak the truth for the Earth. But you can speak the truth for yourself—your truth. This is the voice of the goddess—through you. Find the courage to speak. This is what I would say to every woman in this time.

And to every man?

To every man I would say this: Find the strength to bear the truth of your women. You have been trained not to listen, not to hear, not to recognize. You must change these attributes. Your world and you, yourselves, are in danger of being lost. By holding the reins and not sharing them, you lead the horse of your destiny off in one direction, and you are blind to the outcome. Do not shrink from the shaking earth when your women speak their anger, for the shaking shall set you free—but only if you can bear it.

Listen also to your own heart; the answers to your dilemmas do not lie solely within your mind. You have been trained not to listen to your feelings and to not recognize them as valid or important, but they are a crucial part of your knowingness. Realize that you live because it is a gift from the Earth—the great mother of all things in this world. Recognize that how you are living is harming the Mother. If you can find the strength to bear the truth of your women, this truth will set you free. But if you continue, as you have collectively, to suppress the voice of the feminine, all shall be lost.

The power to open new worlds of beauty, grace, and light lies within the smallest choices you make. The smallest things can have the biggest consequences. Be aware of this and treasure this. Treasure the small things, the small moments of your life, especially in relationship to the women in your life and to the Earth.

What would be the biggest challenge in years to come concerning the divine feminine?

In regard to what is being called forth from the divine feminine, the truth will be at the forefront. The pressures to speak one's truth will increase, and the pressures to remain silent in order to protect one's self will also increase—two pressures in the opposite direction. The destiny of the planet and certainly of Humanity shall be decided depending on which aspect dominates. Will the truth be spoken? Or will silence dominate? That choice is both an individual and collective one. Each person has to weigh, within himself or herself, the consequences of speaking the truth versus the consequences of remaining silent.

Let's put it this way: Humanity and the Earth will survive in some form. But if the powers that would silence the truth dominate, there will be a very difficult outpicturing of negativity in the world for many years before, finally, the truth, the spiritual light, prevails. So by speaking the truth—one's truth—in these times, one brings (forward) the higher destiny sooner rather than later.

INTRODUCTION TO THE HATHOR SECTION
FROM JUDI SION

I thought I might add my two cents worth to the Hathor section of this book as well, since I am the one who transcribes every word the Hathors have said for the past eight years. I first *met* the Hathors through Tom Kenyon. But I had once seen images of them during an odd visit I made to the Midwest where I met a couple who had a Hathor temple room in their old farmhouse. They had images of these beings I had never seen before depicted on all the walls. I was a bit amazed at a room with nothing but images of these beings with a distinctive jaw line, large ears, and Egyptian headdress on the walls of an old clapboard farmhouse standing alone in a vast plane in the Kansas heartland. They suggested I sit for a while in their meditation room, which I did. I must admit no one spoke to me, and I really didn't feel anything during that initial encounter with the images, but I can assure you that I knew I wasn't in Kansas any longer. I remember that occasion, as clearly as if it were yesterday, and it must have been, now, some twenty years ago.

So it was many years after seeing that room full of Hathor images in a Kansas farmhouse before I met Tom Kenyon and experienced the Hathors personally and most directly.

I had heard of Tom Kenyon but had actually never met him and really didn't know what he did. I only knew that he "taught" something, and I had very little respect for teachers by the time I'd heard of him, so I wasn't particularly interested. My experience of many teachers was that they taught one thing and lived another. In fact, my disappointment with teachers had evolved into a life dictum. I felt that the time for the hypocrisy of honoring teachers who carried a body of knowledge but did not live it in their lives was over. And so I had vowed never to be involved with another teacher but to let the rocks and rivers and trees and life be my greater teacher, as they had been in my childhood.

And rather than repeat a story I wrote in *The Magdalen Manuscript,* I'll just say that my first experience of Tom and the Hathors was through a personal reading I arranged as a Christmas present for a dear friend. I wanted something special for this friend, something that couldn't go in a box or be wrapped or duplicated ever again. And when I thought about what to get him, I admit I kept hearing words in my head that said, "Find him the sounds." I tried to hire singers or a band, but no one was in town or available. And then one night in a phone call with a girlfriend, she said to me, "Let me tell you what Tom Kenyon says about the paradigm shift," or some such, and bells went off in my head. I am telling you that bells went off inside my brain, and I asked for his phone number and called it immediately and mumbled something into his business phone about wanting him to be a Christmas present for someone. Minutes later he called me back and asked me what it was that I wanted, and I did my best to explain that I was looking for "the sounds."

He scheduled an appointment with my friend and me. I didn't know that Tom was a practicing psychotherapist as well, or I might have been nervous about what I'd said if I'd known at the time.

And so I took my friend over for our scheduled appointment in a few days. When I knocked on the door, the largest dog I have ever seen seemed to open the door. Merlin had pressed himself in front of the person who stood behind him. We were led downstairs where Tom's office was. Tom invited us into his private office and took out his crystal bowl. I didn't know what to expect, so I sat farther away from my friend, to make sure "the sounds" (whatever that meant) went directly to him. This was not to be my present; this was his present. I sat very still and closed my eyes. Tom began to tone sounds that were beyond anything I'd ever heard in all my life. I'd spent many years in recording studios in my advertising days. I'd worked with musicians and majored in music at one point myself, and no one anywhere in the world sounded like this. I opened my eyes to make sure there was no one else in the room and to try to determine how these sounds were coming out of his throat. It was astounding and deeply altering. I felt myself slipping into a highly altered brain state yet quite aware of my surroundings.

The Hathors introduced themselves and began to tell my friend of a lifetime we had all had together, during the attempt by Ahknaten to change the old priesthood. The story felt deeply familiar, and scenes flashed before my closed eyes like edited movie clips. Emotion welled up in me as the descriptions of the Temple of Isis and the Temple of Ra were given. Through Tom's voice, they made sounds for my friend, and I remember feeling elated that I'd found the sounds I'd been told to find. I had never—and have never to this day—heard anything like the sounds Tom Kenyon makes in a sound session.

And when it was over, Tom turned to me and said, "The Hator goddess wishes to speak to you, Judi." None of us have any conscious recall of what she said, and she has only come through with a group on one rare occasion since that time.

When it was over, Tom walked us to the door. My friend headed for the car, and I was a few feet behind him when Tom called me back.

"Judi," he said, "I need to tell you something." I stepped back closer and he said, "I don't do this."

"You don't do what?" I asked.

"I never see people in my home, and I don't do private sessions."

"Then why did you see us?" I asked.

"Because the Hathors asked me to see you."

At home the sounds haunted me for days and days. I have never in my life, up until that point, been so affected by anything as by that experience with the Hathors through Tom Kenyon. One week later I called Tom again and said, "So if the Hathors told you to see us once before, do you think they'll tell you to see us again? I have a few questions for them."

He laughed and we scheduled an appointment, and that's how it all began.

In the ensuing years, my friend disappeared into the Danish landscape, never to be heard from again, though I still think of him fondly and with great love and respect and hope that someday he may see these words and remember our time together. After Tom's wife died of cancer, we found ourselves literally tumbling headfirst from close friendship into a deeper and deeper heart connection. And though the

Hathors and other deities have said much privately to us, about that time and our life together, we don't choose to share that with the world.

And so it is from the perspective of having "lived" with the Hathors now for over eight years that I tell you what I have experienced in that time.

There is a group of thirteen individuals who speak through Tom. They speak in a group collective, in that there is group agreement on what may be said. They are clearly here as a nonintervening intelligence. They do not use influence, nor do they intervene in any way. Never, not once in eight years, have they ever told us what to do. I have begged for specific information regarding our future and the future of Humankind, and they do not answer such questions. They work on a "need to know" basis.

I'm going to say this again to be very, very clear. A Hathor will never tell you what to do. So if you are hearing voices and they identify themselves as a Hathor, and they tell you what to do in your life or give you directions, trust me, it is not a Hathor.

When invited, they have made *requests* in our life and regarding our work with them. For the past seven years, we have traveled to locations where they say it will be beneficial to anchor sound. We went to Russia because they requested it. We went to the Ukraine because they said it would be helpful to the Earth to anchor sound there. And when we found out how close we were to the Chernobyl, we asked them why on earth they had requested that we visit such a radioactive site, and they explained it was quite purposeful.

They literally said they would have put Tom inside the reactor if they could have, as the radiation would hold the sound for thousands and thousands of years.

I was, perhaps, in retrospect, in the happiest place I have ever been on Fiji, and we wanted to stay longer. But we were expected in Japan, and so we spoke to the Hathors, to see what they felt the ramification would be if we canceled Japan and stayed in Fiji. They explained how helpful the sounds would be to the Earth if we anchored them as close as possible to North Korea, and they requested that we go to Japan anyway and not cancel. This was about seven or eight years ago, when North Korea was threatening to test nuclear weapons and the world was very concerned. The Hathors said they wanted to get the sounds as close to North Korea as possible, and they said it was very important, but, of course, we didn't *have* to go. So we went to Japan, as requested. Only now have they told us how critical it was that we went to Japan on that occasion as things shifted in North Korea as a result, they say.

But all communication is posited as requests to us. It is only when I press them, by speaking directly to them through Tom, that I get the full explanation of much of what they say. It is as if the question qualifies the response in some way, and dialogue adds immensely to answers to specific questions. For example, they have sound temple sites in New Mexico and Central America. Many years ago, Tom considered giving away the site in New Mexico, due to the immense displeasure of working with a board of directors. He went to the Hathors and asked if he could give it away.

They, of course, said yes, he could give it away. They said he could do whatever he wanted to do. I refused to believe there wasn't more to it than that and requested to speak directly to them and asked the next question. I asked what would it mean to the world if Tom gave it away. That got us the answer we needed. It would have been a grave loss if Tom's consciousness and direct access to this group of Hathors were no longer involved with the total control of that temple site, as he is the one with the direct Hathor connection, and for the temple to continue serving the Earth as it does, it is most beneficial to have his input and control. And so we kept the temple site, formed a nonprofit to hold it and to do additional work. Now there is a temple shaft on private land in Costa Rica and one planned for Nepal, to triangulate the acupuncture needle effect the shafts have on the Earth, and the Sound Healing Foundation that we formed as a result has taken on many projects, including the first-ever recording of nuns in Tibet.

In reality, where we go and what we teach in the world is a direct reflection of the requests made to us by spirit, whether that spirit be the Hathor connection or now the deep relationship we have built with the consciousness that identifies herself as Mary Magdalen, with whom we have been working since 2000.

But let me be very clear. Neither the Hathors nor Mary Magdalen ever tells us what to do. They point out what various actions would mean, for both the Earth and for Tom and me. Then Tom and I decide what works in our life after receiving guidance, not unlike guidance from an attorney or an accountant or some other life adviser. (Though, on the surface, there may appear to be very little similarity between receiving consultation from a group of interdimensional beings from another Universe and getting advice from an attorney or an accountant. I can assure you I've received much more valuable advice from them than I've ever gotten from a Human adviser limited to this dimension in their thinking and awareness.) When we are told that our travels are critical to a particular global situation on Earth, we are very glad to do what we can if it works for us as well. We don't connect those dots for people. In fact, we almost never tell people why we accept certain requests and not others.

We don't send our mass e-mails requesting everyone join hands while we sound aum (om) in the desert. We don't announce where we're going or what we're told the sound meditation is about beyond the obvious of helping people who are attending a particular sound session in a workshop. I am not trying to present us as heroes, and I'm not trying to be evasive.

I may simply say this.

In 2007 alone, sound was anchored deep into the Alps of Switzerland, into the Danube in Hungary, and through all its tributaries into all of Eastern Europe. We have also anchored sound in Germany, Austria, France, and Spain. Before we left the United States for this journey of one year, we anchored sound deeply into the United States on both the West Coast and the East Coast. Before we return home at the brink of 2009, we will have brought the sounds of the Hathors from the crypts and Holy of Holies in Egypt, back through

Hungary, to Vienna, France, and then on to Tibet, Nepal, Bali, and back to where they are gravely needed, North America.

I can genuinely say we are honored to be of service.

The Hathors have never been in corporeal form on Earth. They sent emanations to certain artists in ancient Egypt, as well as now, so that their anthropomorphic image could be painted and carved. But they have never had bodies. They exist as light in their dimension. The images in that temple room in Kansas were depictions of how they "showed" themselves to specific artists, and, as with all channeled information, whether artistic or verbal or musical, it is translated through the filter of the evolutionary capacity of that artist, musician, or channel.

This is hugely important in the face of so much channeled material offered in the world today. I've known, for whatever reason, many, many channels in my lifetime. And I can tell you that the clarity of what comes through them is totally dependent on the level of evolution of the individual doing the channeling. They cannot help but *filter* what comes through them. It is inherent. So if I were you, I'd look for a highly evolved Human before I paid much attention to the message. In other words, the medium is very much involved in the message (with apologies to Marshall McLuhan).

In my experience of Tom Kenyon, having observed him both from a distance and close-up now for over fourteen years, he lives what he teaches, every single day of his life. I've never seen him take anything but the "high road" in every single situation he is faced with. He is a genius of immense stature, mentally, musically, vocally, a true Renaissance man. If you spoke with people who know him or have experienced him in either his business or his personal life, the word *impeccable* always comes up. He is distinctly impeccable, a truly honorable, gentle, egoless man. That's another reason I wanted to add my two cents' worth. These are things he would never say, but they deserve to be said for many reasons. They are the truth, and they give you pause to think about the source of all channeled material.

Fame does not equate to either spiritual or emotional maturity, and just about anyone can get a book published, so just because you "read it somewhere" does not make it truth, especially as it refers to "the news" as it is currently "read." (Notice I didn't say "reported." News is no longer reported or proven before being read, nor are there investigators of what is dictated by authority any longer. What is "handed down" is simply read without question or investigation by a talking celebrity head, and what we still call the news bears little or no resemblance to the truth. Be aware and be wary. I'd recommend turning everything you hear upside down, as I often do, and see what the exact opposite sounds like. As Tom often says, filter what you are told through your own personal glasses to see what makes sense for you. Accept what works for you, and discard what does not serve your highest good.

FROM THE HATHORS

We have been told that Sanat Kumara, a benevolent overseer of this quadrant of the universe, invited the Hathors into this Universe. He felt they could be of service without intervention. He specifically invited them to help because of their balanced natures, alchemically speaking, their male/female balance.

In a dialogue with Sanat Kumara on February 6, 2007, he said this to us regarding the imbalance in this universe and the Hathors: "The duality of this universe, with few exceptions, is such that the male overrides the female principal. This is true on other planets and other star systems in this galaxy and in this universe. Thus I requested the assistance of the Hathor civilization because of their balanced natures."

It seems that looking back down the time line, what happens now on this little blue planet at the edge of creation affects this entire universe in the coming decades. He knew that as a civilization they had attained what we had the possibility of attaining: group ascension and balance. They accomplished this by listening to the master teachers of their civilization and all focusing on bliss simultaneously. Perhaps we have/had this potential, but the control and fear factors that have been levied on us in the last few years all but seal our fate to some other method of shifting dimensions, not all of which are going to be pretty. The Hathors say it is possible for us to manage this feat up until the very last second. But the behavior I see among my fellow Human beings does not encourage me to think that we will achieve this potential.

The Hathors are best known for their activities and their depictions in ancient Egypt, but they also tell us that they were heavily involved in Sanat Kumara's activities in a lifetime he had on the island now known as Japan. They also had influence in the early Bon tradition of what is now known as Tibet and also farther south into Africa.

Along with Sanat Kumara, they originally entered this universe some ten and one-half million years ago. They came from another universe, through the portal of Sirius, to Venus, and then to Earth. They were active on Earth before the Hator temples of ancient Egypt, but they are best known from their time in ancient Egypt working through those temples. Hator is/was a goddess to whom the Egyptians gave immense due respect, and a temple to Hator the Goddess was placed in almost every temple complex in ancient Egypt. She was highly deified. She is an individual being, a goddess, not of the Hathor civilization. As is often the case, there was an inner circle understanding, and then there was the picture given to the greater masses. The greater masses came to the Hator temples to worship Hator the Goddess and to ask boons of her. Within the inner circle, the priests and priestesses knew the Beings were different from the goddess. The Hathors work in the fifth through the twelfth dimension of consciousness. Recently we asked the Hathors whose depictions we are left with, since the being known as Hator the Goddess was not of the Hathor civilization. They told us the depictions are of them, the Hathors. Hator the Goddess does not have an anthropomorphic depiction artistically expressed. (Standard Egyptology, however, considers the depictions in Egypt to be of Hator, the Goddess, with cow ears, which they consider a reflection of her fertility aspect.)

Tom has the remarkable ability to "tune" his brain to any frequency and call forth a being. In the case of the Hathors, he recognizes them because they always approach through the heart. After having transcribed what they say, live and verbatim, now for over eight years, he finds them easily and distinctly recognizable. They do not see the world as we do. They say their lowest state of existence is what we would call bliss. They generally live in ecstasy, a state not encouraged for Human beings by either our religions or our government, which is perhaps why we have not evolved further than currently outpictured by our actions in the world.

They were also involved in Lemuria and Atlantis, though more heavily involved in the more heart-centered Lemuria.

They are masters of sound and love, and so it is no surprise to me that Tom Kenyon was chosen to be a source of their information in this time.

Tom can connect to them when he is in a clear state in a matter of minutes. They speak distinctly, and I take down what they say *live*, as it is given. I type quite fast, and they have adopted a Magdalen trait. They now have me read everything back, to determine if it is accurate to what may be presented collectively by them. The Hathor civilization has millions of beings in it, and these are thirteen of the millions. They are master teachers assigned to speak for the collective, rather than just a random group of thirteen, so what they have to say speaks greater volumes than otherwise. They work directly for the highest level of authority within their civilization, and nothing is said that has not been declassified, so to speak.

I find them deeply caring, but not mushy. They are intellectually and scientifically brilliant, and they are funny and see life on Earth as intrinsically humorous. (We figure that's because they don't have to pay rent or vote.)

Though their information is very helpful, it is their sounds through Tom that are life altering and potentially healing and transformative. I see this as simple brain science.

When Tom teaches a workshop, whether it is on Taoism, or Tibetan Buddhism, or Hinduism, or Egyptian high alchemy, or esoteric Christianity, he is delivering a body of information that goes to the left brain of the listeners. They decipher it to their capacity, evolutionarily and semantically. But that information stays in the left brain. It can cause an "a-ha" moment when pieces of dogma are exposed to the light of the truth and people are released from constraints that have held them back. But this experience is a left brain experience, like what is happening when you read these words.

It is sound—pure sound with no decipherable words—that brings the right brain online. Tom teaches this during his sound healing workshops, and it never ceases to amaze me that more people don't see the huge and life-altering implications of such information. This means that when someone teaches with the combination of words and pure sound, magic can occur. This means you have the potential, with such a teacher, of not only understanding what is being taught, spoken, to the left brain but also of having a huge shift, a major transformation, or a healing, or both, during a sound meditation that brings the right brain online. This is what the Hathors do. They use Tom's voice to deliver sound codes that unlock doors and windows of perception, transformation, and healing. This is what they mean when they say they are masters of sound and love.

In eight years, I have never seen them or Mary Magdalen give information that was not correct. I have not seen any information either they or Mary Magdalen have given that was inaccurate. No being from another dimension can every really comprehend time as we have to experience it, but as far as channeled information can ever go in this direction, the Hathors and Mary Magdalen have been very accurate in their postings and timing.

The Hathors began to give what they titled "Planetary Updates" while we were in Hawaii about four years ago, along with their clear instructions about the Holon of Balance, which they continue to say is critical to staying in balance. They say the star tetrahedron is an excellent vehicle for traveling, if traveling through realms or dimensions is your desire. But for balance in the midst of chaos, the Holon of Balance, which is an imaginary octahedron placed around the body, is of excellent use, and they encourage us to practice it, and get comfortable being in it, and be able to place it around us with a moment's notice. They also continue to encourage us to find joy and reside there through ecstasy in the heart.

FROM TOM KENYON

I will tell you what I say to those who attend my workshops: keep an "imaginary box" beside you at all times. If what I say doesn't make sense to you or violates your view of reality, then I suggest you just toss it in the box. Never swallow or accept as truth anything anyone says without sifting it through your own *life experience,* your own sense of *logic* and, very importantly, your own *personal values.*

Swallowing ideas without chewing on them and digesting them thoroughly can lead to a type of mental and/or spiritual indigestion. And for this type of ailment, there is no such thing as an instant antacid.

There are those who say that one should leave one's sense of logic and rational thinking behind when entering into the spiritual realms of experience—that one must fully and completely surrender to faith and not let reason enter into the picture. Personally, I think this type of thinking is dangerous. We need all our wits about us and all the intelligence we can muster if we are not to become deluded on our way to spiritual illumination. It is the true of light of self-awareness that we seek, not the false luminosity of personal fantasy and desire. In this regard, logic and rational thinking are not the nemesis of channeled communications; they are critical allies.

The information you are about to read came to me in a nonordinary manner, via a *channeled state of mind.* I will have more to say about channeling in a moment, but first of all I wish to be very clear that this ability is inherent in all of us. It has to do with an aspect of our being called interdimensionality.

What do I mean exactly when I say interdimensionality? To explain this, let's take a look at it from several perspectives—how interdimensional of me!

As you are reading this or hearing it read to you, the language centers in your brain are making sense of the blabber we call English. At the same time, you might be hearing a sound from outside, perhaps a honking horn or the sound of an animal. You could also at the same moment feel yourself taking a breath. All of these events—the reading of these words, the sounds you hear, and your breathing—are dimensions of consciousness.

You can become aware of any of these dimensions by shifting your attention to them. But it is your attention to an event that

makes it conscious. If you don't pay attention, you won't notice something taking place. If, for instance, you are completely
engrossed in this material, then you might not notice your breath
or the sounds outside. They exist independently of your awareness of them, but in your world of perception it will be as if they
never happened.

Our inner world of perception also has many dimensions or
realms. Most of these are inaccessible to us, most of the time,
because—quite frankly—we have been trained to focus on only a
small bandwidth of internal experiences as significant—namely,
those that make us more productive or useful to society. While
such practical states of mind are undoubtedly important, they
are not the only states open to us.

In order for you to experience these inner worlds of perception, you have to alter your brain activity as through meditation or through some other method. Then you can have a direct
experience of these worlds and the rather amazing phenomena
that take place within you. But until you experience these worlds
directly, it is as if they do not exist because they are outside the
range of your perception.

The ability to access these higher dimensions or creative
worlds within ourselves, although rather esoteric, offers unique
practical benefits. For one, these other dimensions of consciousness can often reveal creative insights and solutions to problems that are not apparent in our normal ways of thinking and
perceiving.

The history of science is full of breakthroughs and new
insights that were brought about due to these nonordinary states
of mind. Let me be a bit more specific here to help explain what
I am referring to.

Science is usually thought of as the pinnacle of Human reason. The scientific method is, after all, based on rational observation and the logical solution of problems. However, in actuality, those who undertake science, the scientists themselves, have reported that at times the solution to a scientific dilemma came to them through nonlogical means.

Take the German chemist August Kekulé, who discovered the molecular structure of benzene. He said that he struggled with this dilemma incessantly. It was an obsession, but no resolution was in sight.

Then one night he had a dream. In the dream, he saw a snake swallowing its tail. He woke up and realized that this was, in fact, the structure of the benzene ring. After translating his vision into the language of mathematics, he was able to prove that his night-time insight had been correct.

One of the interesting things about Kekulé's dream image is that it was a classical symbol out of European alchemy—the *uroborus*.

As a side comment, it is my belief that many alchemical and dream symbols, such as the uroborus, speak to the interconnectedness of matter and consciousness.

The point of this is that the solution to a highly practical problem—namely, the structure of benzene—was revealed through a nonordinary/nonrational state of mind (i.e., a dream).

Thus, significant information can be revealed to us when we enter other dimensions of our own consciousness. The physicist Albert Einstein reported that he uncovered the principles of general relativity through a series of fantasies. And he once quipped that one cannot solve a problem at the level of the problem. One has to go to a higher level to solve it.

The question of dimensions has intrigued physicists and mathematicians as well as metaphysicians for a very long time. The first consideration in regard to dimensionality is from what standpoint one is considering it. Mathematicians, for instance, view dimensions in a different manner than physicists.

One way of thinking about dimensionality, albeit an unusual one, is to think about it as dimensions of consciousness. To begin this discussion, let's consider a book called *Flatland*, written in 1884 by the Victorian satirist Edwin Abbott.

I bring this novella to our attention because it explores the fascinating paradox of how those living in a given dimension can never fully understand dimensions outside their own.

Here is a very brief though incomplete summary.

Once upon a time there was an imaginary world called Flatland. It only had two dimensions, length and width. Those who lived on Flatland were called Flatlanders. No one on Flatland had ever seen anything three-dimensional since Flatland was, well, . . . flat.

One day a sphere (a ball) passed through Flatland. As it made first contact, a single point appeared in their world, which grew to be a small circle. And then the circle grew larger and larger. At one moment, the circle was very large, the largest it ever got. This moment corresponded, of course, when the ball's largest circumference was passing through Flatland.

And then, for no apparent reason, the circle started getting smaller and smaller until it disappeared into a point. And then the point disappeared.

There were many ideas about what had happened, but no one on Flatland knew what had actually occurred. The Flatlanders simply could not imagine anything like a sphere because they could not conceive of anything outside the reference of their two-dimensional world.

I think we are like that.

We live in our day-to-day three-dimensional world thinking that this is all there is. If time is the fourth dimension, as some have suggested, then most of us have a pretty good grasp of it as well. By that I mean we can tell time and can show up at meetings and appointments *on time*. And for most of us that is all we are interested in.

THE PARADOX OF TIME

But there are other ways of looking at time. Our modern mechanistic perception of time is only one aspect, and when we transcend or stop perceived time all together (as in meditation or certain types of esoteric practices), things get very interesting.

Indeed, when we step out from the rut of perceived time (via meditation, etc.), we more easily enter other realms of Human experience. These unusual states of mental and physical being have been described by mystics, yogis, and other illuminated beings for eons.

Their descriptions of their encounters with the *numinous* (a Jungian term for the light-filled realms of being) were, of course, expressed through the cultural filters of their time. Thus, the mystical language of the great Christian contemplatives and mystics are, on the surface, different from those of their Judaic and Islamic cousins. And certainly these descriptions are even more dissimilar from their Asian counterparts—Hindu and

Buddhist yogas, and the Taoist alchemies of China. But beneath the surface of their apparent differences, there are deep currents of similarity.

The similarities that I am speaking of here are *not* related to belief, spiritual lineage, or dogma. Indeed, many mystical traditions are in complete opposition to each other on fundamental points of dogma. In spite of these differences, there are striking commonalities in regard to the methods these mystical and yogic disciplines employ to enter the numinous. And the alteration of perceived time—whether attained through meditative trance, contemplative prayer, or chanting—are central to all these traditions.

Indeed, we could say from the standpoint of modern neurophysiology that it is through their alteration of perceived time (and its attendant changes in brain state) that all yogis, mystics, and saints apprehend what they call the Divine, the Transcendent Self, or the Tao (depending on their intellectual and philosophical bent).

In other words, mystical and religious experiences occur (neurologically speaking) due to distinct changes in brain processing. Please note I am not saying that mystical experiences can be reduced to and are the sole result of physical changes in the brain, but such experiences are definitely characterized by simultaneous events in the nervous system. This may sound like splitting hairs to some, but for those of us involved in the pursuit of scientific insight into mystical states of mind, it is crucial to be as rigorous as possible.

My personal conviction is that the numinous realms of being (i.e., mystical experience) open to us a fascinatingly rich area of

Human potential, but only when the imprisonment of dogma (religious and/or cultural belief) has been stripped away.

From the standpoint of neuropsychology, channeled information is just another expression of our brain/mind's potential—similar, in some ways, to mystical states of mind.

Channeling is not, however, a religious act. Rather, it is a movement into the unknown territory of one's own psyche (the numinous) to see what emerges in terms of *contact* (with other intelligences) and *information* (in the form of new insights).

As a psychotherapist and as someone who was involved with brain research for over ten years, I regard channelings in general as a type of *transpersonal psychoartifact.*

Indeed, from my perspective, channeling is simply the art of shifting brain wave activity in distinct ways, which, in turn, generates transpersonal experiences and information.

THE PROCESS OF CHANNELING

Anyone who channels does so by altering his or her awareness in some manner. The result, regardless of the method used, is that the channel enters into a deeply altered state or *internalized awareness* (trance). For the time period of the *communication*, one is more or less detached and somehow suspended from one's normal ways of being in the world, including one's perception of perceived time. This is a direct result of changes in brain state (i.e., an increase in alpha and theta activity on the part of the channel).

As exotic as the channeling state may sound, I believe that it is an inherent ability that most, if not all of us, possess. It is simply a matter of learning how to voluntarily change one's own brain state.

But there is another element in the channeling phenomenon that is critical for us to understand. It is the question of filters. I personally don't think that there is such a thing as a totally clear channel. We can approach being a *clear and open channel* and hopefully get ever more impeccable, but *the Presence or Information* that presents itself through the channel is somehow affected by the channel—especially by his or her emotional state, subconscious beliefs, and *miasmas* (toxic personal distortions).

This unavoidable filtering of information in the channeling state is why I said earlier to always have an imaginary box by your side. If some part of a channeled message doesn't make sense to you, toss it in the box. Don't accept it as truth. Test it through your own sense of logic, your own life experience, and your own values.

It is my hope that those of you who read these messages will do just that. See what works for you. Toss out the rest.

One of the worst things that could happen with this information, in my opinion, would be to *deify* it in some kind of New Age cultism. Instead, look at *the messages* simply as information from another dimension of consciousness, a unique perspective on our world, one that will hopefully allow you to be more resourceful and happy in how you deal with your life.

FROM THE HATHORS

We are the Hathors. We come in love and with the sounding of a new dream reality for your earth. If you are ready to build the new world, we invite you to join us on a journey of the mind and heart. We are your elder brothers and sisters. We have been with you for a very long period of your evolution on this planet. We were with you in eons past—even in the forgotten days before any trace of us is known in your present written history. Our own nature is energetic and interdimensional. We originally came from another universe by way of Sirius, which is a portal to your Universe, and from Sirius we eventually proceeded to your solar system and the etheric realms of Venus.

In the past we have specifically worked with and through the Hator fertility goddess of ancient Egypt. We also made contact with Tibetan lamas in the formative period of Tibetan Buddhism. Although we have interacted with some of Earth's early cultures, we are an intergalactic civilization with outposts that span parts of your known Universe and beyond. We are what you might term an ascended civilization—a group of beings existing at a specific vibratory field, even as you have an energy signature. It is simply that we vibrate at a faster rate than you. Nonetheless, we are all part of the mystery, part of the love that holds and binds all the universe together.

We have grown as you have grown, ascending to the One Source of all that is. We have grown in joy and through sorrow, as have you. We are, in terms of the vastness, a little higher on the spiral of awareness and consciousness than you are; therefore, we can offer you what we have learned as friends, mentors, and fellow travelers on the path that leads back to remembrance of All That Is.

We are not saviors; we're not messianic. We want to clearly step out of that projection so that the reader understands that we are simply elder brothers and sisters offering our understanding and what we have learned. You may take it or leave it, but we offer it freely. In our understanding, the belief that different alien intelligences are going to save you is just a projection of Human unconsciousness. The hope that someone or something will save you, that you will not have to make any changes in yourself, that you will not have to be responsible, is unrealistic. The belief that you can stay in patterns of lethargy and unconsciousness, then take something or have something given to you that will transform you without any effort on your part, is sheer folly. It won't happen. Now, there may be alien intelligences that land, for they certainly exist, but those Humans who count on others to bring in their ascension and elevation without any work on their part are going to be very disappointed. Ascension is a process of self-awareness and mastery on all levels, and it necessitates bringing all those levels of one's existence upward. That is how we see it, and that is how we have done it for millennia.

By offering our aid, however, we do not wish to interfere with your other spiritual helpers and cosmic relationships in any way, or with any religious beliefs, affiliations, or organizations of help to you. Even so, there is a great deal we would like to share.

We know Sanat Kumara well for it was he who asked us to enter this Universe. As an Ascended Master, Sanat Kumara has taken on numerous responsibilities associated with the elevation of planet Earth and this solar system. He is working for the ascension, the evolution of consciousness in the solar system, as we are.

We wish to convey to you today that you are at the brink of tremendous change, and the world as you have known it is in the process of birthing into something new. As your world enters the stages of birthing into higher dimensions of existence, much that you have taken for granted will no longer be. The portal of time through which you must pass is now upon you, and the acceleration has unquestionably begun.

This moment in time is a rare and precious opportunity. We speak not of the *little self,* the personal self, but of the *greater self* that you are. This greater aspect of you, this interdimensional reality that you are, receives an immense evolutionary catalyst through the act of embodiment in these times. The *greater you* is beyond time and space, as you understand them. The personal you is like one facet of a complex jewel with many faces. The experiences you create for yourself in this world add to your understanding and the depth of your being from the vantage point of your greater self.

There are many forces in your world. Some of them are striving to contain you and continue to imprison your mind, your heart, and your spirit. But their deathlike grip on you and your destiny is loosening, for even they are having trouble riding the waves of accelerated time.

If there was one message we could convey to you at this time it would have to be this: *Live in the fullness that you are.* Do not be deluded by the illusion that you are a small, limited, insignificant Human being. Those who wish to control Humanity's destiny would perpetuate this. We say to live from the fullness that you are—your interdimensional nature—for through these higher aspects of yourself you will discover new solutions to the problems that face you. The doorway to this interdimensional reality of yourself exists beyond the constraints of time, space, and history. You are not bound by them unless you will it so.

The doorway to this reality of yourself, to the freedom that is your nature, lies in something very simple. It is so simple, it is forgotten, and there are those who would tell you that the solution cannot be something so seemingly insignificant. But through this almost-secret door you will find yourself in a world of immense freedom and insight, even if those around you are seemingly imprisoned and in conflict. For the world you live in has less to do with your physical location than it does with your spiritual vibration. The door that we speak about is called joy. Happiness. And so our message is quite simple. We have offered, and will continue to offer, techniques, inner technologies, to assist you as you move through the great birthing, but everything we say can be reduced to this one simple truth: *Find a way to live your life in joy and happiness.*

The Hathors

Thirteen

THE POWER OF SOUND

THE SINGING REVOLUTION

I heard a fascinating story recently about a movie called The Singing Revolution. *This revolution was a strategically nonviolent movement by Estonians to end decades of Soviet occupation. The Estonians figured that as long as they shed no blood, the Soviet government (Gorbachev at the time) wouldn't be able to send tanks to decimate the demonstration. So people of this country sang. At one point, a million of them were singing at once. It seems pretty incredible to me how a simple act like singing could have such an effect! I understand that singing was not the only factor, but it seems to have been a very important one.*

How can sound have such a powerful effect on a situation? What goes on at a vibratory level?

We will not comment on the specific event in Estonia, but we can comment on the principles of sound in regard to a situation like this.

First of all, the Human voice has an innate capacity to communicate emotion, thought forms, and subtle energies. When the voice is aligned with *intention*, the sound has a power that it does not possess otherwise.

When you gather two or more people together, you have, alchemically, what is called the third force, which means that there is a third energy beyond the individuals. It is a "joining" of the "powers of intentionality" generated by each person. So if you have a group of hundreds, or thousands, singing a song that is known by each person, with a common intention, several phenomena can take place, and these could explain the sudden departure of tanks and troops.

We will look at this from three levels.

First of all, *the third force.* This is like an individual who does not possess a body; it is an energetic phenomenon. It is created by the intentionality and the sounds, the songs sung by the individual persons. But the third force is a collective gathering of energy, and it has a palpable force that affects individuals in unique ways. It can impart courage and strength and determination. It can also, depending on the intention behind it, crack open a closed heart. And, indeed, soldiers undertaking military action, by necessity, must close their hearts. Otherwise they cannot impart violence to another of their kind.

And so if you have a thousand people singing the same song with the same intention—especially if this intention were non-violent—the third force generated would pierce the armor of the hearts of those who were gathered to attack. Some of the soldiers would experience an opening to their hearts sooner than others of their comrades—for the setting aside of the armor of the heart is an individual action, and some are able to do it sooner than others.

The second aspect of this involves *interdimensional physics* and is a result of the third force interacting with a probability in the future. This is a rather arcane subject, and we will try to simplify it. If soldiers were sent to a location for the purpose of attack, a probability would move down the time line into the near future where such an event was more likely to take place.

Because of the nature of the third force, which paradoxically is created within the constraints of time, in this case by those who were singing a song, the force itself operates outside time. Because the intention was nonviolent, the probability would proceed down the time line and encounter the probability of attack by the soldiers. The two intentions would interact creatively in a vortex of interdimensional energy, something your science is just beginning to understand.

The third aspect of this has to do with what we would call the *highest self* of each person. This aspect is "outside" time and space but can affect events in time and space in direct ways. This higher aspect of the *self* is entered when one is in a state of love, compassion, and nonviolence. It is a distinct vibrational range of consciousness. If one person were to stand in front of tanks, it would not have the same effect. It is only when hundreds gather together, joined in a common intention of compassion and nonviolence, that the higher expressions of themselves would reveal themselves.

For soldiers, in such a situation, it would be peculiar to suddenly have the shade that was drawn—the shade that obscures the light and their connection with their fellow Humans— pulled up and to see themselves holding weapons. That would be surrealistic. The essential point is this is that it would be an individual act of each soldier to place down his arms, to allow the third force and the higher expressions of *self* to affect him. And it would be a creative moment in time where a song, a sound vibration, joined with intention, specifically the intention of nonviolence and compassion, changed a probability from a catastrophe into a blossoming of the Human spirit.

SOUND AND HEALING

Moving beyond the 4D affects the biology greatly, to say the least. It is different for each person, but one thing that many Lightworkers seem to have is ringing in the ears. What exactly happens when this takes place?

Sound and healing is a very complex affair. We shall endeavor to break it down into its components, but it is the combination of all components acting simultaneously that give sound its power as a healing modality.

The first level is well understood by your neuroscience and is a result of sound striking the ear, creating changes in the brain through the auditory pathways. This alters brainwave activity, neurotransmitter response, sympathetic and parasympathetic response, and cascades down into every organ and system of the body. We would say, however, that the sound vibration proceeds down into every cell, though your science has not yet affirmed this.

Another component of sound as healing technology is the fact that audible sound affects the energy field of the body, what the ancients call the aura. Your science is also looking into this phenomenon in the field of subtle energy medicine. Certain types of sounds, especially when joined with intention, can affect the energy field in dramatic ways. This energy field of the body envelops every cell.

Moving deeper into the phenomenon of sound, we turn our attention to the interesting relationship between sound and light.

Essentially, from our viewpoint, what you call material reality and all of the various forms of energy that your science has named are expressions of one fundamental phenomenon: the interchange between matter and energy—energy into matter. Thus, at a very subtle expression, sound generated in a particular way strikes the continuum of light.

To explain this, think of an imaginary piano. It has the eighty-eight keys that are normal, but it also has keys way beyond eighty-eight. If a pianist were to hit the notes above the eighty-eighth key, it would become light, and you could create a chord of light as you would a chord of sound, and what you would see is different colors of light. But you would not hear it because it would be moving too fast. But if you were to take that cluster of notes in the high range of the imaginary piano and play those notes within the normal range of eighty-eight keys, you would hear a chord; and there would be a direct relationship between the sounds you heard and the colors you saw.

When sound is articulated and generated from a high level of understanding and mastery, it can cause energy to step down into matter or matter to step up into energy.

Let us be a bit more specific. It is possible for sound generated in this manner to strike a tumor and to transform the tumor from its physical form of matter into light, into energy, and the tumor would disappear.

It is also possible to bring something that is missing in the physical body at the atomic level—at the molecular level—by activating a pattern in the realm of light and shifting energy into matter. This is a very advanced mastery of sound, but it is one of its potentials.

What we mean by "something missing" is the entire continuum of the physical body in form. It is easier to bring into expression a molecule or an atomic pattern; thus, a hormone

could be brought into the body that is missing from the continuum of light, or crucial neurotransmitters. The principle is the
same when you move into the clustering of molecules and the
organization of organs, but it takes much greater mastery and
skill to replace an organ from the realm of light than it does to
replace a molecule. But as we said, the principles are the same.

As Humanity enters a higher expression of its spiritual
nature over the course of the next century—in spite of evidence
seeming to the contrary—there will be sound healers who are
able to do this. And, indeed, you will find in the coming years
a renaissance in medicine relating to the use of sound in all
its applications, and by that we mean both technological and
Human intuitive, meaning a person using her or her voice to
affect healing.

RINGING IN THE EARS

In regard to ringing in the ears, there are several reasons why this
can occur. One reason is simple neurological deterioration in the
eardrum and the inner ear canal.

A second reason has to do with processes in the auditory
centers in the brain, and your science has recently begun the
process of separating the two: what they call tinnitus, as generated from nerve degeneration, from tinnitus caused by changes
in the brain.

There is a third reason (for ringing in the ears), which has to
do with the energy field of the body.

As individuals evolve spiritually, their *field*—the aura, as
the ancients refer to it—goes through many changes. There

are, within the field, many pulsating smaller vortices of energy. You may think of the auric field as a large luminescent egg that completely surrounds the physical form. Within this luminous egg-shaped form are all sorts of geometries and formations of light. When any of these become activated due to intergalactic, planetary, or personal evolutionary reasons, these areas vibrate at a different rate than they did previously, and sometimes it sets off a response in the brain that is heard as an external sound. It is often a single note or a small series of notes that will repeat themselves.

One method for dealing with the phenomenon of ringing (in the ears) is by making it the focus of your attention. This will help if the reason for the ringing is caused by changes within the brain or the field. It will not affect the ringing in the ears if it is nerve degeneration.

In this method, you simply listen to the sound or sounds. After a few minutes, the sounds will change or disappear. Ideally, you would take a few minutes to focus your entire attention on the sounds, and you would notice that another series of sounds would emerge. These sounds are more subtle. And if you listen to these sounds, a third set of even more subtle sounds will become apparent to you. In other words, you can "ride" these sounds into ever more subtle levels of awareness.

Using this method actually allows you to trace the pathway of subtle sound to a place of absolute stillness. There are ancient yogas that deal with this knowledge, and in India it is known as nada yoga. From our perspective, there is a great deal of dogma and lineage attached to this knowledge. Separating the dogma from the knowledge, we would like to say this. All beings—Human, animal, plant, and otherwise—all possess vibrational fields of energy because they *are* vibrational fields of energy. The smallest subatomic particles vibrate and oscillate, and if you have the technology, you can bring these sounds, these vibrations, within the Human range of hearing. You would describe them as songs, although very unusual ones. Within your Human body, your scientists have estimated you have approximately one trillion cells that are made up of an even larger number of atoms and molecules, and every bit of matter sings with its own vibrational song, and so you are in a very real way a walking symphony—although some of you are more harmonious than others.

In the process of spiritual evolution, one's mental and sensory attributes become refined. Which aspect of you becomes refined depends on many factors, partly your own constitution and spiritual nature, the culture you find yourself in, and the religious taboos that exist. Some individuals will find their sense of spiritual light increasing. In other words, they see colors that are not physically present. Others will find their sense of hearing going through a process of refinement. These individuals could easily be hearing an increase of external sounds.

What we wish to say to those who are hearing external sounds is to think of these sounds as artifacts of their own energy field, so that you are witnessing a vibratory expression of your own energy, your own physical being. From our perspective, this is the first primitive sign of clairaudient abilities, the ability to be aware of psychic auditory impressions.

Although you did not specifically ask this in your question, since we are on the topic, we wish to include those who are experiencing an increase of kinesthetic or emotional awareness.

Just as someone may evolve clairvoyantly, meaning with increased spiritual vision, one can also evolve clairaudiently, meaning with the spiritual capacity to hear, or clairsentiently— with the ability to sense things physically that are of a spiritual nature.

For these clairsentient individuals, this time poses unique challenges, for a clairsentient person might also be called an *emotive responder,* an empath, an empath who senses emotional feelings of those around him or her. This is part of the clairsentient ability.

As this world passes through the portal of radical transformation, there are many individuals who will become distressed, upset, and irrational. This is caused by the simple fact that the world as they perceive it is changing in ways that are not in their control. This creates distress for most Humans; thus, an empath would be receiving broadcasts from many individuals in distress.

And, indeed, for empaths who are evolving rapidly, this can be even more of a difficulty, because it is possible to become a *planetary empathy,* by which one senses the empathic waves of the entire Earth; and by that we mean such a person could be flooded with emotions and feelings from the collective Humanity and also from the animal kingdom, for the animals on your Earth are in great transition as well. As for certain empathic and clairsentient individuals, it would also be possible to receive empathic information from the Earth herself, Gaia, as living goddess energy materialized as Earth. Indeed, for such a person, these times would be most challenging.

We have a suggestion for those who are emphatic in nature and moving toward clairsentient capacity: It is vital that you find a way to separate your own feelings from the feelings you receive from those around you. This is the primary fundamental critical development that must take place for all empaths and clairsentients; otherwise, it can be very distressing to be in these times. Another way of placing this in context is to say that you must be the *sovereign of your own reality* and be clear about what is your sovereign reign, or right, from those around you. For an empath or clairsentient, clarity leads to freedom.

Having addressed the challenges facing an empath in these times, let us offer some specific ways of dealing with it. Let us be very clear here. Those reading this information may not at this moment be empathic. They may be weighted more to the clairvoyantly (psychic seeing), clairaudient (psychic hearing), but eventually the clairsentient ability and empathic response will develop in all Humans. So while this information may not apply to you today, it may very well apply in a few months or a year. And if you survive this passage in your present body, you will certainly have empathic responses on the other side of 2030; somewhere in there the bulk of Humanity will have emotional psychic ability.

What do we mean by this? It will be very difficult to tell a lie. It depends on the evolution of the individuals, as in all things. So within this time frame we have given, some individuals will be highly psychic on all levels, clairaudiently, clairsentientally, and clairvoyantly. For these individuals it will be absolutely impossible to pull the wool over their eyes, so to speak. However, lesser-evolved Humans will, by this time, have discovered an emotive evolution. Their empathic or clairsentient abilities will have increased enough for them to sense when they are being lied to. Unlike a highly developed clairaudient/clairvoyant/

clairsentient combination, meaning possessing all three psychic abilities, someone who is simply empathic may not know the details of the lie but will know with unswerving certainly that he or she is being lied to. This is why politicians, as you currently know them, will be a thing of the past, like the dinosaurs.

So we turn our attention to a few simple suggestions for those who are finding an increase in their empathic response to the world. This could be the topic of a book, but we will try to distill it down to a few essential points.

What we would say is that empathic individuals may find it most helpful to deal with their own geometric structure and personal emotional signature. What do we mean by this? Essentially what happens for an empath is that all the doors are open to the world, and everything and anything, both elevated and distorted, can come through the doors and into the house, so to speak.

For certain empaths there is an impression from other lifetimes, a vow that was taken, to be open to the world. For many this vow was taken in Lemuria, for the Lemurian period was a time of dealing with the world through open-heartedness, unlike the Atlantians, who deal with the world through the mind, disconnected from the heart. So the challenge for those in body now, who were healers in Lemuria, is that times have changed, but somehow the soul or essence has not recognized this. For in Lemuria the advanced healers received their healing powers by having all the windows and doors of the house of the *self* open. And then they could receive empathic information about the person needing healing, and they could receive the knowledge from the higher spiritual realms of what was needed to heal the condition.

The essential requirement for these types of Lemurian healers, metaphorically speaking here, was to have the house of the self open to the cosmos, and to the world, and to the person needing healing in front of them. In other words, there was no window, door, or opening that was closed. From our perspective, in this time, that strategy is counterproductive, because the culture that was Lemuria is long gone, and this culture in which you now live is highly toxic, and it is not advisable to have all the doors and windows to the house of the self open to this world in this time.

So our first suggestion to such individuals is to know that you have the ability and the right, the sovereign right, to close the doors and windows of your self when needed. This is the quintessential paradox for highly developed empaths, because for such individuals it is difficult, and even painful, to close the openings to the world. It runs counter to their nature. But they must find the way to recognize when they are in a toxic situation, meaning people or situations that are not in their best interest, because to take in the energies of such people or situations becomes a toxin, a negative energy in the body of the empath.

So our suggestion is this. Close the windows; close the front door and the back door. Close the cellar door. And when someone knocks at the door, you take a look before you open. So that is the principle.

What this has to do with the geometric structure is this. The auric field of an empath is open to the world. It's as if there are channels literally running into the luminous egg that are connected to the outside world. We would propose to empathic individuals to experiment with the geometric structure that we call the Holon of Balance, and indeed, we suggest this structure to all individuals who are evolving at this time. You will find the complete instructions on how to create this Holon of Balance a little further in this book. But because the Holon is a specific platonic solid, it imparts balance. It is very comforting and pro-tective for empathics, for empaths. What you will find is that the Holon of Balance does not close you off from the world but provides a permeable boundary, which is what is required, from our perspective, for mental, spiritual, and emotional health.

In regard to emotional signature, empaths must become intimately aware of their own authentic emotions or feelings, separated from all others. This then becomes a compass, and this is what they should follow when they are crossing the sea of many conflicting emotions. But only if they have learned how to recognize their own personal authentic response and use that as the compass, can they ever hope to cross over the sea of turmoil that is generated by Human emotion, especially in these accel-erating times.

We have spent an inordinate amount of space discussing the empathic response because, as we said earlier, all Humans are go-ing to find an increase in this ability. Indeed, one could describe the spiritual process of evolution as being centered around the opening of the heart, and as the heart opens empathic response increases, and the boundary between love for one's self and love for the world goes through a change. From our perspective, anchor-ing one's self in the truth of one's own being is crucial. Whether you are clairvoyantly evolving, meaning that your psychic seeing is increasing, or clairaudiently evolving, meaning an increase in your psychic ability to hear, all persons must eventually deal with their own empathic response to others, and how you do this is the great adventure of spiritual mastery.

Fourteen

THE HOLONS

THE HOLON OF BALANCE

We suggest you experiment with this, play with this, and master this very simple geometry. Carry it with you in your conscious awareness at all times so that you may create it at will, as needed, both for yourself and those you are connected to.

It is called a Holon, and the specific one we refer to is the octahedron, or the Holon of Balance. Imagine yourself surrounded by a pyramid of light that extends above you and a matching pyramid below you. These are square-based pyramids, one pointing up and one pointing down. You are in the center of this. If you are lying down, you are on the square, where the two halves of pyramids touch, and the pyramid above you matches the pyramid below you. You make this as large or as small as you wish, so long as you are completely enclosed within it.

If you are standing or sitting, the axis of the octahedron extends through the center of your body, so that if you were to draw a line through the apex of the pyramid through the center down to the apex of the opposite pyramid, this line would pass through the center of your body. This octahedron balances energy. It is the balancing of the male and female aspects of consciousness. Do not let its simplicity fool you. It is a powerful tool for balancing subtle energies.

Do the Holons produce a sound?

No Human could grasp the sounds made by the Holons. That would be impossible to reproduce at the current level of technology and understanding.

Do Hathors work with Holons?

We do not work with Holons because they are part of our natural innate geometries. We created the Holon of Balance and the Holon of Healing as tools for these times that we impart to our Human brothers and sisters.

SOME OBSERVATIONS BY TOM KENYON

The octahedron is one of five three-dimensional geometric shapes known collectively as the Platonic solids. The octahedron has a total of eight sides, thus the root *octa*, meaning "eight." The top pyramid has four sides, the bottom pyramid has four sides, and the bases of both pyramids meet to form a square. The Platonic solids can be found occurring naturally in nature, especially in the form of crystalline structures, as well as atomic and molecular configurations. Esoterically speaking, each of the Platonic solids has specific energetic effects. Some people have e-mailed us and asked if the octahedron is the same as the star tetrahedron, and no, it is not. The star tetrahedron consists of two triangular-based pyramids, and they are not joined at the base. They merge into each other. The star tetrahedron also has different energetic effects from the octahedron.

When I first received information about the Holon of Balance from the Hathors, I thought it was pretty simplistic. But sometimes the simple things are the best. There is no doubt in my mind that this Holon imparts a feeling of balance and protection when it is engaged.

FURTHER ELUCIDATION
ON THE HOLON OF BALANCE

To clarify the Holon of Balance. First of all, this information is for those who may need a more basic understanding of this particular Holon (the octahedron). It is not intended for the advanced student of sacred geometry. I have purposefully kept this simple. And the reasons are twofold. For one, you do not need to have a complex understanding of the Holon of Balance in order to use it. And two, many people are turned off by complex geometries. Since this Holon is highly effective and simple to use, I have chosen not to complicate matters. In other words, I choose not to go into detail about the subtleties between the various Platonic solids or the intricacies of working with them esoterically.

Here is a little sketch of an octahedron, since sometimes a picture is worth a thousand words.

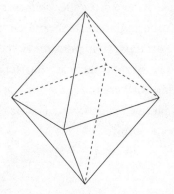

An octahedron is basically two square-based pyramids joined at the base. The Holon of Balance is created by forming an octahedron of light around you through the power of your imagination.

It doesn't matter what color you make it. The color may change spontaneously, depending on your state of mind. Personally, I make mine clear white light, but that is a personal preference, not dogma. In fact, there is very little dogma around this, thank God, thank Goddess.

The main thing is to make sure that you are completely enclosed in the space of the octahedron. If, for instance, you are lying down, the base of both pyramids (where they meet at the middle of the octahedron) will most likely be right underneath you. But you could put yourself anywhere inside the geometry. You could hover up at the top, or sink down to the bottom, or slide over into a corner. It doesn't matter. And you don't have to orient yourself to any direction in particular, like north, south, east, or west. There are also no prayers, incantations, or special breaths required. The whole affair is quite simple. And this may be one of its many saving graces, besides the fact that it works.

If you are standing or sitting, the axis of the octahedron (i.e., the imaginary line that runs through the top of both pyramids to meet at the center) would, most likely, pass through the central axis of your body (running through the crown at the top of the head, through the perineum). But you could imagine yourself up near the apex of the top pyramid or down at the apex of the lower pyramid. In other words, the central plane of the octahedron— the place where the two pyramids meet to form a square—could be aligned anywhere on your body. Perhaps you will have it aligned with your heart, or maybe your head, or perhaps your feet. It does not matter—at least as far as its balancing effects are concerned. In actual fact, some alignments of the center square with your body (i.e., where the square passes through you) may affect you stronger than others. So I say—experiment! Find out what works best for you. Although I am being redundant, let me say it again: It doesn't matter where you put yourself in the octahedron, where you orient it, or what color you make it. The main thing is to make sure you are completely inside it.

One final point about the geometry: Is the octahedron the same as the star tetrahedron? No, it is not. They are distinctly different geometries. Since I am purposefully not going into the details of the differences, if you are interested in further information, I suggest using your Internet search engine to explore the fascinating worlds of geometry and its complement—sacred geometry. There's a whole world of information out there just waiting to be discovered. And it's all at your fingertips with just a click of your mouse!

In a past message, the Hathors gave some information about sending the Holon of Balance to places or persons in distress—in order to impart a balancing energy. In this instance, creating the Holon of Balance (octahedron) is very similar except for the fact that you are obviously not inside the Holon—the person, persons, or area of the world you are sending the Holon to, is inside the Holon. In other words, if I send a Holon of Balance to an area of the Earth, I imagine this area inside the Holon.

You can send these Holons of Balance anywhere on the Earth you wish or anywhere in the universe, for that matter (if your belief system takes you there). Sending Holons of

Balance is a kind of benevolent act, but there is a caveat—don't mess with other people's reality. In other words, everyone has a right to his or her own suffering. Just because you or I would like someone to be in a more resourceful state doesn't mean that they want to be. We all have a right to be sad, angry, confused, or whatever, for as long as we want. Sometimes it gets a bit fuzzy. Maybe we have a friend or a family member in distress, and we want to make things better. But to project our intentions on others when it is not what they desire is, I think, a misuse of subtle energy. And so my suggestion is to send the Holon of Balance not as an imperative or an imposition but as an invitation, a breath of fresh air, so to speak. If we send a Holon as an energetic offering of balance to those who choose to accept it, without attachment that they do anything, then we are, I think, sending Holons into the world in the right manner.

My suggestion is to make learning how to create the Holon of Balance a game. Play with it. Spin it, maybe. Make it different colors. Find where it feels best to you to place yourself inside the geometry. Practice it at odd times in the day. Create the Holon of Balance in all types of places. No one will know what you are doing. Do it when you are shopping, taking out the trash, feeding your pet, taking a walk, or during commercials when you're watching TV. The list of where and when you can take a Holon break is virtually endless. The thing is to practice it enough so that when you feel off-centered—emotionally or energetically off-keel—you can, without thought, create the Holon of Balance. Then it becomes a great ally. It will be one of your best friends, and unlike a dog, you don't have to feed it or take it for a walk, and it won't chew up your newspaper.

THE HATHORS RETURN . . .
THE HOLON OF IMMUNITY

Due to the destruction of your ecosystem and other repercussions of the misuse of your technology, bacteria and viruses are mutating at a record rate, and new forms are appearing. This Holon has a powerful effect on your immune system. It is not meant to be a substitution for taking care of yourself, but it is an adjunct; and if you find yourself getting ill, this Holon can be of great benefit.

Essentially, it is a cylinder that runs around you, from just above your head to just below your feet. At the top of the cylinder the shape bends forward like a banana, facing to the front. At the bottom of the cylinder, the shape moves in the opposite direction from the top. So if you were to look at it from the side, it would look very much like a banana that had been twisted around. Some call it the dolphin Holon. You sense this shape around your body, holding the impression that it is a silver color, very much like a silver Mylar balloon. This silver color does not need to be seen but only needs to be imagined. It is specifically related to the antibacterial and antiviral properties of colloidal silver. Sense this Holon around you, and when your mind wanders, bring it back to the sense of the Holon. This specific geometry causes the subtle energies within you to be calmed and at the same time energized in a specific way that strengthens the immune system. We suggest you add this to your "first aid kit," so to speak.

Is sound better absorbed by our consciousness when we are asleep and the mental aspect has surrendered somewhat? If so, how much more effective is it during our sleep?

We would say in terms of passivity, receiving sound while sleeping is probably superior to listening to sound when you are awake, on one level. However, this is a lower level of reception.

Our understanding and our methods involve conscious co-creation between the receiver and the sounds. In other words, it is the focus of your mental attention on the sound vibrations that creates the greatest transformation. Certainly, for a small minority of persons, their own personal issues get in the way, so to speak. Their distortions, their egoic conflicts, may prevent them from aligning with the sound when they are in a conscious state of awareness. For such individuals, listening while going to sleep is a good method, but generally speaking, it is far superior and leads to a greater level of mastery to take the responsibility for co-creation. Using your mental focus—your full attention—on the texture and pulsation of the sound creates cascades of effects throughout many levels of your being. This is the superior way of listening to all types of sound that are intended for healing.

Within the context of conscious listening and co-creation— meaning when you listen to sound with your full attention— there are several phenomena that take place. One of these has to do with the alignment of the sound frequencies with specific locations in the physical body or the energy field. If you are consciously paying attention to the sound, you may discover its resonance within your body or your field. If this occurs, place your awareness in the pulsation in your body or field, as well as on the sound. This is a very powerful catalytic way of listening.

There are many states of consciousness that arise when consciously listening, including, paradoxically, states of seemingly deep unconsciousness. It is as if you are listening and then

suddenly you are *gone*. No awareness of the sound. No awareness of your self. Perhaps there is a sense of having gone somewhere but not knowing where, or it could be simply a "blackout"
period, where one enters into a deep state of unconsciousness,
but it is not sleep. There are several reasons for this. Sometimes
individuals transit to another domain or realm of their being,
and when doing so, they enter a state of quasi-unconsciousness.
This is because they do not have a bridge, so to speak, from their
conscious awareness to other dimensions of themselves. And so
the sound vibrations may generate a response in the individual
that causes him or her to travel to these other realms of themselves, and for this time, they have no awareness. When they
return to awareness of the body and the sound, they realize they
have been unconscious.

At other times, the sound will create a very low or slow
wave activity in the brain that your scientists call delta. This is
the realm of sleep. As the individual responds to the sound, if
the sound carries them inward, meaning into their inner worlds
of perception, there will be an increase of threshold brain activity
your scientists call theta. This is the place of dreams and visions
and transformational imagery, and as you move into these lower
states of theta, you are at the threshold of delta, or sleep. So for
some individuals, the sound causes them to go inward, and part
of this process takes them into unconsciousness. We would say
this type of unconsciousness is a state of processing within one's
own nervous system and is not a transiting or traveling to other
realms of one's being. So there are many states and phenomena
that can arise in response to sound, especially when listening to
it consciously.

I've been thinking for a while now about sound and pregnancy. When a child come in, he loses so much of his interdimensional aspect that I was wondering if sound could help in any way in lessening that fact. I know that when a child is born, he is still very connected to the divine and that connection slowly disappears at a conscious level.

In the last trimester of pregnancy, the fetus clearly receives sound vibrations through the auditory channels of his or her brain and nervous system. Prior to this, the auditory channels are not sophisticated enough to fully discriminate subtle differences. However, the energy field of the developing fetus is highly responsive to sound and vibration as well as emotion, we might add—specifically, the emotional state of the mother. The energy field of the adult is also highly receptive to sound vibration, but generally speaking, children's fields are more permeable, less structured, and less rigid.

From our understanding, the reason a child loses his or her contact with the divine, as you have stated (or, as we would say it, *interdimensional* aspects), is due not so much to a lack of support during pregnancy but, rather, enculturation. During pregnancy, the child is in the environment of the mother. She is like a Goddess to the small developing embryo, and the embryo floats, so to speak, in the great uterine sea, and his or her world is enclosed by the world of the mother. So her emotional responses and her thought forms are very powerfully *impactful* and are a global aspect of the embryo's reality.

At the moment of birth, however, the newly born child leaves the environment of the mother and is suddenly in the world, and his or her highly permeable energy field reaches out into the environment and is deeply impressed, shaped, and formed by what he or she encounters. Children, by nature, have an open heart, but in the process of contending with the culture at this time, they learn how to close it or disconnect from it. So the loss of interdimensional contact is a cultural phenomenon.

When our children are born to us, we gather shortly after the moment of birth and sing what we call the *Song of Highest Destiny*. It is done with the intention of clearing the obstructions for the child, sending the sound vibrations of our voices down the time line of this being. We find it highly nurturing, supportive, and, in retrospect, effective at helping the child come into our world.

What we would suggest in terms of benefit to a child before birth would be for the mother to sing to the embryo and, if the father is available, for him to sing as well. There are a few suggestions here. This should be a lullaby that comes from the heart of the mother or father. All that has to be done is to make contact with your authentic feeling of appreciation for this child. If you do not have authentic appreciation for this child, then we suggest you do not sing to him or her because then there will be a mismatch between your reality and what you are trying to communicate through the lullaby. Singing to the child from the moment of conception onward has a positive effect, if it is done in this way.

For those who are aware enough, there is another element you can add. This is a more subtle use of intention and thought form. As the mother or father sings to the child in a lullaby-type way from the heart of appreciation, hold the thought form or belief that the sounds you are making open pathways into the interdimensional or divine aspect of the child and clearing the way into the future. This is an advanced form of communication, and if you are capable of doing it, you will immediately understand how to do it from our brief description. If what we are saying is a quandary for you, don't worry about it. Simply sing to your child in a lullaby from your heart, with appreciation.

It would be a wondrous gift to this world if all children were brought into this Earth realm in this manner.

Fifteen

THE SPIRITUAL CENTER AND CROP CIRCLES

Our spiritual center seems to be one of the most important things to have in preparation for the years to come. But for some reason, it is difficult to find and easy to lose when you have it. Why is that? Is it simply a lack of will or discipline?

When one finds one's spiritual center, the true center point of one's being, nothing can move one from it. What occurs is that people approach their center, and with each level of proximity to the center point of their being, there is an increase of peace, certainty, and fluid stability. What we mean by this is the ability to be both stable and fluid as required in any situation that one encounters in life. So one may get closer to one's center and think that one has found it, but as the times increase volatility and chaos, the stable ground, so to speak, wavers and then one says that one has lost one's center. But we would say, "You have never really found it." Because once you find it, it cannot be lost. There are other factors here.

From one perspective, we could say that there is confluence to discourage one from locating one's center. Religions and social institutions lead one in the wrong direction if your goal is to find your center. For some people, finding the center point of their being is not a goal. But for those who have entered this life experience for the purpose of transformation, finding one's spiritual center becomes important. So it depends on whether one's goal or focus in life is external or internal. For those who are directed solely externally, such a center is of no interest.

You mentioned in another text "Crop circles are signatures, a living record of an interdimensional conversation between Earth and interdimensional visitors." Could you elaborate about this "conversation"?

Regarding crop circles, and focusing our comments on true and authentic crop circles, meaning those not created by Humans, our experience of them is a delightful conversation between Earth as a conscious being, whom you call Gaia in some circles, and the many cosmic visitors. These include intergalactic intelligences as well as interactions with the energies of deep space that are passing through the solar system at this time. So some of the crop circles are messages from the intergalactic visitors. Some of them are responses from the Earth back. Some of them are related to the past history of the Earth. Some of them are an attempt to wake up the Humans—to see in the patterns the complex information that is being offered regarding your glorious destiny if you will but shape it.

It is very interesting, energetically, to watch the movement of information from Earth through the grains, or the plants, or the substances that create the circles. But the forms are becoming much more complex over the years, and this is because the conversation between Earth and the intergalactic visitors and the cosmic waves are becoming more intricate. As this phenomenon increased and the conversations became more complex, more of the devic kingdoms began to participate, and so it is that the plants themselves, the living biological forms that bend to create the crop circles, are not passive, but part of a dynamic process between the intelligence of Earth, the intelligence of the "cosmic visitors," so to speak, and the willingness of the devic kingdom to participate in creating a record of the conversation. If there were no physical record of the conversation, very few Humans would have any idea that such a conversation had taken place.

So now you are left with a growing series of complex geometries. These geometries are a language, and you stand looking at it, much like the early Egyptologists looked at hieroglyphs and did not comprehend their meaning. But even though the meaning was not understood, it was still there in the hieroglyphs, and we would say that this is the stage you are at in relation to the crop circles. It is a planetary and intergalactic language.

If you wish to explore this, we would suggest you look at the visual photographs of the crop circles as they were first documented to the present and observe the changing complexities. Meditating, if you will, on the images can allow you to enter into a beginning understanding of this language.

We realize that such information gathering is highly personal and relative to the evolution of the individual. There is, unfortunately, no Rosetta stone in this case (a carved record that allowed Egyptologists to translate hieroglyphs). In many regards, in relation to Humans, the crop circles are an intelligence test. We can offer a few suggestions for deciphering the deeper meanings of these geometries, these records of a conversation.

Look into two levels. Atomic structure, including the bonding into molecular structures, is one level. The other level is intergalactic and cosmic in proportion—in other words, the microcosmic, meaning the atomic/molecular level, and the macrocosmic, meaning the cosmic level. The geometries, especially the ones that have emerged in the last few years, can be overlaid upon certain atomic molecular structures as well as configurations of stars, galaxies, quasars, nebulae, black holes, and the other astronomical features of the Universe. In other words, this conversation taking place is multidimensional and deals with changes and transformation at the very atomic and sub-atomic levels, all the way into galaxies and all the astronomical features of your universe. It is a very complex conversation.

Sixteen

ECSTASY OF THE HEART

We wish to speak with you in this section concerning the generation of ecstasy through focusing on the heart. We do not speak of the heart chakra in this instance, but, rather, we refer to the physical heart, the heart muscle itself.

This technique involves your focus, or attention, joined with the emotion of gratitude, or appreciation—whichever term you prefer to use. As soon as you focus your attention on the heart, you may notice a flow of subtle energy.

From our perspective, your focus of attention operates much like the central point of an energy vortex. This is especially true within your physical body and the field surrounding your body— your energy field—what the ancients called the aura.

Your ability to create a focus of attention is not just a cerebral, or brain, activity. It is an activity on many levels of consciousness. Wherever you place you attention within your body, or within the energy field of your body, there is an immediate flow of subtle energy to that point, or area, which has an enlivening effect on the cells of your body and/or the luminous light fibers that comprise your energy body.

Your focus, indeed, creates a warping effect at the subatomic levels, what you might call quantum field effects. These field effects create distinct flows of energy, geometry, and harmonics within you.

To alter the quantum field through the power of your focus is an important ability we urge you to master. Its applications are numerous, the cultivation of ecstasy being just one of them.

In this method, you use this ability to hold focus or attention, joined with the emotion of appreciation or gratitude. These two emotions have a coherent effect on your energy field and on the rhythmic magnetic emanations of your physical heart. This combination of focus and coherent emotion can be used to generate high states of ecstasy.

As we have said previously, the generation of ecstatic states of consciousness is an important evolutionary catalyst. We strongly suggest that you learn to create states of ecstasy throughout your day.

We realize that, for many of you, your daily life may not be conducive to the cultivation of such states, but we urge you to find times throughout your day where you can practice attaining these states for at least a few minutes at a time. A little bit of time spent in ecstasy is better than no time at all.

This practice will set up a harmonic or a relationship with the Earth, as a conscious living being, and with the harmonic waves of catalytic evolution that are flowing through your galaxy.

In this technique, you focus your attention on the physical heart. As you focus your attention on this area, you generate the feeling of appreciation or gratitude. It is not the thought of appreciation or gratitude but, rather, the emotion. In this method, thought will not activate the subtle energies needed to generate ecstasy—only feeling is capable of activating the energy vortices within you.

As you focus on the physical heart and generate the feeling of appreciation, or gratitude, a waveform of energy begins to flow throughout the body—carried by the magnetic fields of the heart, which emanate outward from the physical heart to encompass your entire body. As the flow of energy begins throughout the body, there is a spontaneous arising of ecstasy—cellular ecstasy.

Experiment with this technique. Sense what happens in your body as you focus on your heart and generate these feelings of appreciation and gratitude. Physically feel what seems to be happening at the cellular level as the one trillion (or so) cells of your body receive this coherent energy of gratitude or appreciation.

Once you have established the ability to create ecstasy as described here, and once you are able to generate ecstasy whenever you desire it—at will—begin to experiment with your energy field—what some call the subtle energy body.

In working with this method, your attention is, again, on the heart, generating feelings of appreciation and gratitude. And as you sense ecstasy beginning to arise in your body, you shift your attention to the field around your body. This field of energy looks very much like a luminous egg when viewed clairvoyantly. The wide part of this luminous egg shape is up around the shoulders, and the more narrow part is around the feet. There is a central line or axis that runs through the center of this field, and it happens to also run through the center of your physical body—through the top of the head and down through the perineum. This line is the central axis of the magnetic field that comprises the subtle energy body. This body, or field, extends above the head and below the feet a few inches, to several feet or even yards. In certain highly charged energy states, the axis and subtle energy body can expand much farther than that.

By shifting your attention to this central axis and to the field surrounding your body, you allow the ecstasy to move out from the physical body into the field. This is very positive and creates powerful harmonic patterns that bring you into resonance with the waveforms of accelerated evolution that are flowing through your galaxy.

Do not underestimate the powers of this technique. Though it is very simple, it is profound and effective. It will bring you into a higher state of resonance and vibration. And this is, from our perspective, crucial in order to pass through the energetic portals and transformational energies that your Earth is now experiencing and will continue to experience.

There are things we would like to say to you about your nature and your destiny, but they would, most likely, not be understood by you unless you are, at the very least, in a state of ecstasy.

This is because the reference point for consciousness is established not only by belief but also by one's emotional harmonics. And without you being in a state of ecstasy, it would be like trying to describe a sunrise to a blind person who does not have the ability to directly perceive what you are talking about. To such a person, it would be a make-believe world you are describing. But if suddenly this person could see, he or she could sense the sun directly and verify that your description of the world was accurate. And what was once deemed to be in the realm of myth would now be seen as real.

And so we leave you in this moment with what may seem like a myth but that we hold as self-evident. You are creator beings in the midst of creating your future and the future of generations yet to come. You hold within your heart a key to the Mystery of Mysteries. And the threshold, the opening into this mystery, is through your capacity to enter ecstasy. Be bold and find your path, your way of living upward, into this elevated state of being. Do know, however, the ecstasy is not the end of the way. It is simply the beginning.

Try the method we have laid out for you here. Experiment with the methods we have given earlier and that we will give in the near future. Enter ecstasy whenever you can. Know that when do so, you enter into communion with all the elevated beings and masters who have served and who are serving Humanity. Know that when you do so, you enter into communion with your Self.

Seventeen

THE YEAR 2009 AND BEYOND

Before going into the core of our message, we would like to elaborate on two subjects: the weather and going beyond the American influence in the world.

The first principle we wish to convey regarding weather is that it is mitigated or affected by collective Human consciousness in a way that is not currently understood by your science.

Your science looks at the physical causation for changes in weather, and indeed, this is a primary factor, but what is not recognized at this point in your time line is that you are co-creators of your multidimensional reality, including your physical experience of Earth.

So looking down the time line, let us say that you possess free will and can change anything that is seen in the future. What we see are probabilities—but it is only when you arrive in the present moment that the probabilities collapse and the reality emerges. So your "choice points" all along the time line are important moments of power. In other words, you can change what we are seeing.

Having said that, we expect to see an increase in volatility of weather. In some areas there will be extreme drought and in other areas extreme flooding, as in 2007. There will, most likely, be an increase of tornadoes in areas of the world that have not experienced them previously. We expect to see an increase in the strength of hurricanes and cyclones. There is not an area of the world that is immune to these weather anomalies.

We have spoken before about the Ring of Fire, and this Ring of Fire extends energetically from the northeastern areas of Russia; through Siberia; down through China; into Japan; down into Indonesia, Australia, New Zealand; up into the west coast of South America, Central America, and North America; ending off the coast of Alaska not very far from its origins off the coast of Russia. This is the primary *resonating* ring, and from here there are energetic lines that affect other earthquake-prone areas of the world.

There are complex grid relationships between the Ring of Fire and other fault lines. These include apparently unconnected lines that run through parts of China, India, Pakistan, and into Turkey, Greece, and Italy. Your geological science has not found a direct relationship between these because they are subtle in nature, but in our way of viewing Earth energies, we see a direct relationship, not so much through the classical fault line structures but through harmonic relationships between the various levels of the Earth, such as its crust, and the lower levels extending to the mantle. These harmonic relationships are driven not just by the tectonic plate movements but also by solar activity. This is an energetic phenomenon, and the sun is in an increased period of activity that we see continuing for several years, at least.

We expect, however, to see an increase in earthquake activity and intensity worldwide. That also includes unexpected Earth activity on the East Coast of the United States and Canada. But we would say that these are not necessarily reasons for alarm and fear. These changes in the Earth are an expression of her changes, and, indeed, earthquake activity has existed for millennia. We include in this volcanoes. There are some who look at projections of Earth changes in the future as a form of self-torture, to perpetuate fear, but if you understand that the phenomenon that we are talking about is affected by consciousness, it is possible to ride through an earthquake and an intense weather pattern and have it be a catalyst for rapid evolution. It is all in how you *deal* with the situation, not the situation itself.

AMERICAN INFLUENCE IN THE WORLD

One of the probabilities that we spoke to in earlier communications was a downturn of the U.S. economy. We indicated that November 2007 would be the most likely last window where this would take place, and, indeed, it has unfolded as we had seen it. As we look down the time lines, the probabilities are high that American influence in the world will decrease over the next decade. This is due to economic and political reasons, and during this time other countries will step forward, but in the short term, American influence will be very strong in the world, even as there is a decline in economic power and influence.

What will emerge in the next decade, politically and economically, is that those countries that turn their attention and emphasis on the personal individual, on the true taking care of the environment and the natural resources—those countries that are "wise stewards"—will prosper, and those that are not will experience difficulties. So, again, we see consciousness affecting outcome. As we move into the next decade, we expect to see an increase of spiritual evolution, or at least what might be called planetary community.

In this new sense of the world that will grow in the Human family, old ways of politics and economic domination will not be favored. While the world will not move toward a place of equality between nations, at least in the hearts and minds of the planetary community, this will be a clear ideal and one that many will be working toward.

The preparation we would advise is to recognize that you are a co-creator of what is happening around you. You are not passive, although you may feel "acted upon"; even your passivity is a form of active creation—creation by not taking responsibility. We would say that in these coming times, it is vital to recognize your sovereignty as a creator force, to avoid the mind control and manipulation of those currently in dominant places of power, to use your own mind to sense out the truth and not trust what is told to you, for you are surrounded by lies. You must use the highest levels of your own heart and mind to ferret out the truth of every situation. You must come to recognize that your heart and mind—your thinking and your feeling natures—are powerful forces that when combined together become a creative dynamo. You are at the threshold, collectively, of a new world. How difficult the transition of this birth will be depends largely on you and all your fellow Humans.

Recognize that it is a grand adventure. Whether you survive a particular period of this transition physically or not is immaterial from the standpoint of the greater being that you are a part of; for your current embodiment is like one facet of a diamond, and how you deal with your life, with the incredible moments of these times, strengthens you or weakens you. But it is not the situations themselves that strengthen or weaken you, but how you create your response to them. This is your greatest power. And no power on Earth can take that from you. When you know this, you are invulnerable. And what we mean by this type of invulnerability is that when you are in this place of personal power, it is immaterial to you whether you live or die, for you have found your spiritual center and recognize, with full certainty, that you are a spiritual being beyond the constraints of time, space, and history. You are a being of luminous light having a Human experience.

TRANSCEND AND TRANSFORM YOUR WORLD

We wish to speak with you about a perilous passage in which you now find yourselves. Much of what we have said in our past communications has come true. From what we have told you just earlier, you will see even more Earth changes, climatic alterations, geopolitical destabilization, and threats to the ecosystem. These will unfold in the years to come.

But that is not the perilous passage of which we speak of now. We are, rather, speaking to your emotional life, the life of your heart and your spirit, for it is unquestionable that the unfolding events of the next few years will emotionally strike those who have sensitive hearts and who dream of a better world.

We would divide our comments into two areas: transcendence and transformation. When the chaotic phase of re-creation begins—which is the phase you now find yourselves in—all structures come into question. Destinies that have been calculated based on expected outcomes dissolve. It is a time of immense confusion, and the primal emotions of fear and hostility arise. There are several forces at work in this, and we wish to discuss them.

Part of this chaotic phase is the simple result of the shift from one dimension of consciousness to another. As Earth and Humanity move from fourth-dimensional consciousness to fifth-dimensional consciousness—which is outside the constraints of time and space as you collectively perceive them—there is a tension between the old world and the new world. You are right in the midst of this.

As more and more people experience paradigm shifts driven by sudden leaps in spiritual understanding, the old world is undermined. The new world with its new cultural, political, and economic presuppositions has not yet blossomed, so you are in a kind of no person's land where the old views no longer work, but the new views have not yet come into usable expression. So this is one reason for the difficulties you are experiencing in this dimensional shift.

But there is another, more insidious element at play here as well. There are vested interests that wish the old world of domination and control to continue, and they are using every means at their disposal to insure it.

The type of control we speak of is so pervasive and so much a part of the fabric of your society that it is often overlooked—which is exactly what those who wish to control you work toward. There is no one person or group of persons responsible for this type of control. It comes from many directions and sources. It comes from sources you might never suspect, including religious, political, and economic institutions. But the attempts to control you do not end here. Many of the manipulative elements in your world are also coming from interdimensional and intergalactic interference.

But regardless of their source, the days, so to speak, for those who are trying to control your destiny for their own selfish ends are numbered. The shift from fourth-dimensional consciousness to fifth-dimensional consciousness cannot be stopped any more than the dawn of a new day can be avoided. The evolution of consciousness on your Earth and of Earth herself is in the midst of a dynamic shift, and you are a vital part of it.

However, we wish you to understand that the transition from your current fourth-dimensional reality to the fifth dimension (and higher) is not going to be an easy one. Due to the inherent chaos that occurs during a dimensional shift and due to interference with your world from terrestrial powers, as well as from interdimensional and intergalactic intelligences, the transition will be much more difficult.

This is not to say that you cannot lessen the negative events in your future by actions you undertake. But it does mean that a graceful collective transition to higher dimensions is probably unlikely.

We have always avoided sharing information that is alarmist in nature, but we also need to be direct and honest in our assessment.

Throughout the recent past has been both an intensification of the dimensional shift and an increase of planetary manipulation and control. This parallel event—the shifting upward into the preludes of fifth-dimensional reality (the foyer of higher planetary consciousness, to use a metaphor) and worldwide attempts to control and contain the Human spirit will be paired off in a virtual and real tug of war. Indeed, this war for the Human spirit has already begun.

There is not much that one single person can do to mitigate Humanity's collective destiny. But by stepping out of the collective mind control and manipulation that is hypnotizing the world at large, you have the possibility of affecting your own destiny in distinct ways.

In order for you to do this, you must find a way to transcend your own limitations, and by this we mean the limitations of your thinking, which have been imposed by your institutions, your governments, and your religions. You must find ways to transcend the messages of fear and terror projected into Human consciousness by the events that are unfolding before you and by the manipulators of these events who are unseen. If you are to survive this period, you must transcend what is happening, or seeming to happen, around you. You must find your own spiritual center. We explained earlier this principle.

There are no magic ways to do this. Each of you has several pathways that will lead you to the still-point of your own consciousness, to the realization of your own divinity; and from that place, you can more easily detach yourself from the events that unfold around you. You will have learned to transcend the world. One of your great spiritual teachers once said, "Be in the world, but not of the world." This is very good advice in the coming times that are now upon you.

But it is not enough to simply detach yourself and transcend the world. You must also transform the world, and we speak not here of the greater world, for that is beyond your ability to affect. We mean the world right around you, your local community of friends, loved ones, and the Earth that is actually beneath your feet. This is the world that we speak of, and this is the world you must transform even as the greater world seems to deteriorate and fall apart all around you. This shall take a great degree of spiritual mastery. We are not saying that it is or will be easy, but we are saying it is absolutely imperative that you transcend and transform your world, both together—simultaneously—in order to pass through the eye of the needle.

And so when you find yourself disheartened at the state of the world, our advice to you is to transcend this self-indulgence, to transcend the manipulation and sense of isolation that is being projected on you, to transcend the group mind form. This is tricky business because you must find your own path into the joy of your heart, even in the midst of suffering that may be around you. There will be times in the coming years when spiritually sensitive individuals will feel the desire to give up. This is the time to reinspire yourself, and how you do this is up to you, but we do have a few suggestions.

Turn your attention away from yourself and your own problems to the world around you, to the Earth underneath your feet, to your local community, to your friends, to the strangers who live around you, to your loved ones. Discover what you can do to make that world in which you live a better place. These things are very simple, actually. It could be a smile, a comforting word, offering a space for a car making a turn in front of you; it could be offering food to someone who is hungry; it could be turning off your television mind control device and playing with your children or your pets. It could be planting a tree. The list of opportunities to affect the world that is right around you is endless, and then you will find yourself reconnecting to your local community, even as the forces that would manipulate the world try to destroy it.

Do understand that there is power in simplicity, which is why our messages usually deal with simple basics. As always, we suggest you cultivate the Holon of Balance as a highly effective way to deal with energetic instabilities as they arise We also encourage you to live consciously in appreciation or gratitude, for the subtle harmonics created by these emotional states will act as protectors for you and lift you up even if the world takes a downward spiral.

Seize the moments of your life, even if your culture and your economies go through difficult times. Find the space within your self to detach and transcend what appears to be happening around you. Then you will, perhaps, have a most interesting experience. You will see the cosmic joke, and the entire affair on your planet will appear to you as both an interesting and amusing transition into higher consciousness.

This sense of amusement is, however, only seen, of course, from the vantage point of fifth-dimensional consciousness and higher. It is not always easy to see the innate humor of situations as they arise in a dualistic universe—especially when you are locked into it. This is why we encourage you to transcend your world—the world as you believe it to be—and to enter into a higher octave of awareness. A new universe brimming with possibilities awaits you.

We are the Hathors.

Eighteen

THE MAKING OF A VERY SPECIAL CD

TOM KENYON

The whole affair began in a most unexpected manner. I was answering questions toward the end of a Sound Healer's Training in Seattle, Washington, in September 2005. A woman raised her hand and said that she worked with AIDS and HIV patients in Africa through a nonprofit organization. She asked if I had any recordings or sound patterns that would help, as the situation was getting quite dire throughout that part of the world. I replied that I did not have anything substantive to offer, as my psychoimmunological work up to that time had been centered on general immunity and nothing that specific.

She then said that she had a request, a challenge, actually. I recall the moment clearly as the room suddenly filled with a spiritual presence when she spoke. "I have a favor to ask of you. I know you are very busy, but Africa is in distress, and I know you can help."

The thought of adding one more thing to the list of growing projects I had committed myself to boggled my mind. I was about to stammer out something to this effect when I clairvoyantly noticed a being standing off to my right. He was an African shaman who was adding his weight to the request. And then all my guides came to me, and the stage was suddenly very full. I heard myself say, "I will find a way to create the time to do this."

Mind you, I had no idea how I would ever pull this off, given the fact that I was easily working fourteen to sixteen hours a day on other recording and writing projects. I was running on empty, as the saying goes, plus Judi and I were in the midst of packing for another world teaching tour.

About four days after this encounter, I was awakened at three in the morning, by my group of thirteen Hathors. They said that now was the time to begin working on the immunity program. They said it would be pure vocal sound, without the use of any electronic frequencies, and would be channeled with the assistance of spiritual healers from many diverse realms of consciousness. They also informed me that most of the recording would usually take place around 3 A.M. since this was the time of least interference from collective thought forms—including my own. They put me on notice, in other words, that I would not be getting much sleep for the next few weeks.

In fact, it took four weeks to record all thirty-two tracks, each of them consisting of a different being channeling his or her spiritual light into audible sound. It was an exhilarating and mind-expanding experience that kept pushing the edges of my own personal paradigms and beliefs.

The first two tracks were laid down by the Hathors. These tracks, I was told, would be of assistance with many types of cancer in addition to HIV/AIDS and other immunological problems. I was also told that the final recording would address immunity on many levels—not just physical, but emotional and spiritual as well. How it would accomplish this feat was not clear to me at the beginning, but as the recording process unfolded I began to see the larger picture. Immunity is not just the physical response of our immune systems to immunological threats. It is both the biological sense of self and the spiritual sense of self-identity.

After the first two tracks, the vibrational energy of the spirit healers changed considerably. An African shaman appeared to me clairvoyantly and indicated that he wished to offer the assistance of plant spirit medicine, meaning that he called on the spirits of specific plants to help alleviate physical and spiritual illness. I knew about this type of healing and had experienced it myself on two separate occasions from two different practitioners. This way of working with plant spirits seems to have long traditions throughout much of North and South America, as well as Africa. This form of medicine may have traditions in other parts of the world as well—it's just that I am not familiar with them.

What struck me about this shaman/healer was that he had obviously not been in a body on Earth for a long time since many of the plants he used for healing were no longer physically present in Africa. They had long ago become extinct. For a moment he seemed to be in grief and disbelief. And then I watched him traverse the stars and the spirit worlds to find his spirit brothers and sisters (his plant medicine) in other realms of consciousness. He then called on them and brought their spirit medicine back to Earth in the sounds that he sang through my voice. When I finished that sequence, I was sobbing from the power of the energies and from the pathos of what I had just witnessed. I stepped out of the recording booth to find a large African male standing etherically in the studio. I recognized him as a Masai warrior. He bowed, and we communed for a few moments in silence—him thanking me for keeping my promise, and me thanking him for his visitation.

Over the years, I have become quite used to channeling many different types of spiritual energies and beings in the course of my work. But I had never channeled so many diverse types of energies in such a short space of time, and the experience was deeply altering to my perceptions of the spirit worlds.

Some of the beings who sang their healing from the realms of light into the world of sound were recognizable to me—lamas from Tibet, healers from ancient Egypt, India, and Persia. Some of them were alchemists of the highest order, and some of them were creator gods and goddesses from ancient times and places we have no names for.

About a third of the way into the recording process a group of angels began to download their healing codes. Each of these codes had specific geometries of light associated with them, and as each angel sang through me, I was elevated to such heights that I would literally stagger out of the recording booth when I was done with his or her sequence. Some of these angelic beings I recognized from Christian and Islamic traditions.

But some of them were unknown to me. My only sense of them, besides their majesty and power, was that they had been sent forth from the heart of the Divine to aid in the immense task of planetary healing.

I will never forget one session, about halfway through the recording, in which I witnessed the Tao sending forth a form of pure chi (or life force) from the Formless Heaven into a sound pattern. The sound seemed to be not of this world but, at the same time, deeply healing. Every cell in my body was both comforted and nourished by these primordial sounds. During one session, I watched as the Blue Medicine Buddha called forth an exquisite form of healing light from the Sambhogaya (the Tibetan realm of pure light and sound). I watched as he wove the light together and lowered its vibrational frequencies from that of spiritual light into spiritual sound.

In one session, a Mongolian shaman called on the horse-headed god of healing known as Hevajra by Tibetans. As I saw Hevajra manifest within the realms of light, I saw thousands of wild horses running across the plains of Mongolia—a potent symbol of the primal healing power that was being released through these sounds.

In other sessions, Native American shamans and healers would sing and call forth healing powers through their intention. One in particular affected me deeply—Buffalo Calf Woman—a legendary figure of immense healing power. Her tones shook with a potency that left me in both amazement and appreciation of the feminine power to heal.

For twenty-eight days, in the early hours of the morning, these extraordinary and diverse beings joined together in one common purpose: to release to the world a form of healing and potential at a time of desperate need. Spiritual lineages that rarely meet and were often in conflict in this world were joining together to create a healing power that left me stunned and speechless.

Toward the end of the recording process, both Magdalen and Yeshua added their voices to the healing choir, and for me, this was both calming and integrative in its effects. Throughout the recording, I would listen to each new voice as it was added to the previous ones. There were a few times when the sounds were too catalytic, too strong and volatile. They left me, and those listening, shaking from the release of too much personal negativity. With the addition of Magdalen and Yeshua, the release of negativity was still present, but with a sense of comfort and stability. A fertile ground for healing was completed. All that was required were the seeds of intention that each listener will sow as he or she listens to the codes. It is now quite clear to me that this unique psychoacoustic program is a cocreative matrix. It is an auditory trail of spiritual light whereby the healing intentions and energies of these spirit healers can be joined with the intentions of those listening.

THOUGHTS ON IMMUNITY, BELIEF, AND HEALING

I have come to see immunity in a much larger context than just our physical immune response to pathogens. From a biological perspective, our immune systems are a way to determine self from nonself. If something invades our bodies (e.g., a bacteria or a virus), our immune systems quickly ascertain if they are a part of us or not. If they are not recognized as a part of our personal biology, then our immune systems mobilize their resources to destroy the toxic invaders.

Physical immune response is a very complex affair—a combination of many factors including genetics, nutrition, environmental factors, personal vitality, as well as mental/emotional patterns. This last aspect of immunity is often referred to as psychoimmunology or psychoneuroimmunology. This field of research looks at how our thoughts and especially emotions affect our immune systems. And while such ephemeral things as thought and feeling are only one small part of the immune puzzle, they are an intriguing and important aspect.

On a practical level, if you wish to enhance your immune function, you need to be conscious of and improve the quality of your air, water, and especially nutrition—the food you eat. Regular periods of rest have also been found to be important for good immune function. These periods of health-inducing rest are characterized by increases in alpha and theta brain wave activity. Certain types of meditation are ideal for generating these kinds of stress-reducing brain states. Research has shown that those who meditate twenty minutes once or twice a day tend to have better immune function and wellness than those who don't.

But the type of immunity of which I speak is not just confined to the physical response of our immunological systems. This larger context for immunity is an expression of what I call our vibrational signature.

Our vibrational signature (or tonality) is related to our emotional life—specifically, what we are feeling at any given moment, and especially habitual emotions that are an everyday component of our own personal thinking and feeling habits. Conceptually, I place various feeling states into one of two categories: coherent emotions or incoherent emotions.

Coherent emotions are feelings like love, appreciation, peace of mind, gratitude, and so forth. Incoherent emotions are feelings like hate, jealousy, a sense of lack, mental agitation, and the like. Most people generally prefer to experience coherent emotions because they have a coherent effect on their bodies and minds. Incoherent emotions make us feel uncomfortable because at a subtle energy level, they are disruptive.

There are some fascinating studies that show how incoherent emotions (like hostility, for one) can negatively affect our physical immune response and even heart rhythms. But the jury is hardly in—scientifically speaking—when it comes to how and to what extent our health is affected by our emotional lives. So I do not wish, at this time, to get into a discussion about the psychological and physiological mechanisms of physical immunity.

The type of Immunity I want to focus on, at this moment, is the larger context I mentioned earlier. From this metaphysical perspective, we are being bombarded every day by all types of toxins and pathogens. But these toxins are not confined merely to the physical realm, where science, by necessity is focused. This type of contamination also includes what I call mental, emotional, and even spiritual toxicity.

When we are lied to by someone, by a group, or by a society, this is a type of mental, emotional, or spiritual toxin. These forms of misinformation have a long history and tradition, including the types of misinformation that exist within family systems, societies, and cultural and religious dogma, not to mention misinformation disseminated by governments and corporations. The whole idea is rather mind-boggling, so I will do my best to simplify some of the basic concepts.

Let's take families, to start. In an ideal family (which, by the way, does not exist), the relationship between the parents is balanced, and their children incorporate this balance within their own psychological makeup through the process of growing up and interacting with these two ideal parental figures. But in real life, there is rarely a balance of power. One usually has the upper hand and wields it over everyone else. In the fascinating kaleidoscope that is Human experience, the domineering parent might be direct or passive in his or her manipulation of power. One might be a raging bull when he or she does not get his or her way, scaring the you-know-what out of everyone in the family. Or he or she might be what some have referred to as a "subtle tyrant" to get his or her way.

Subtle tyrants are passive-aggressive and never meet a situation head on with honesty and directness. Their bids for power are executed in the shadows (meaning the unconscious—either their own unconsciousness and/or the unconsciousness of those around them) and often with an overlay of helplessness and guilt. Some use illness, for example, or the threat of illness as a means to get what they want.

As children growing up in a family system, we unconsciously metabolize and accept the underlying beliefs (thought forms) about life, relationships, and the world—as well as our place or lack of place in it. The emotional patterns we see depicted before us as children also become incorporated as part of our being. Usually we incorporate such emotional and thought patterns as our own, or in some cases we rebel against those patterns and beliefs. Such a person often runs the risk of being perceived by family members as a black sheep—the one who refuses to conform to the family's beliefs and expectations.

If a belief or power manipulation in the family runs counter to the authentic nature of one of its members, this creates immense psychological and even physiological conflict in the one who is out of step or not with the program. In some families, mild rebellion is tolerated—up to a point.

In some families, however, everyone has to hold to a very rigid standard of mental and emotional life. For instance, cutting or not cutting one's hair can be a big issue in some families. Dating or even having friends with someone from another religion, cultural group, or race can be met with hostility in others. And some children have found themselves disowned because they chose a different career than what was expected of them.

My point in all of this is that our beliefs (thought forms) and emotions become a part of us through a process of mental and emotive metabolization. In other words, our thoughts and emotions become part of our very flesh. The constitution of our bodies is not just formed from the food we eat and what we drink but also through what we think and feel.

The coercion to make us think or feel in certain ways is, I believe, one of the greatest detriments to our spiritual, mental, and cultural evolution. Whether it shows up in our families, with friends, at work, in our places of worship, in how we contemplate or hold the divine within our minds, or in our political institutions, the mechanism of toxicity is the same.

When we are forced or expected to think and feel in certain ways—against our nature and our own best interest—this can become a form of mental or emotional toxicity. For some of us such toxicity can be worked out, but for others it festers and creates either physical illness or, in some cases, what I call spiritual illness (meaning that the vitality of our spirit has been dampened, suppressed, or depleted). I believe that in the next few decades, science will have a lot to say about this process of mental emotive metabolization—or how our thoughts and feelings become physical—but for now such concepts are on the fringe, to be sure. But then, to be frank, so is this entire immunity recording.

For some, the idea that spirit beings could come through someone's voice and sing healing codes that will actually help a person must seem preposterous. For others, it just makes sense. It all depends on where you are coming from in terms of your own beliefs about reality and what is possible—not to mention your own life experience.

I had to continually expand my own perceptual box while working with these spirit healers because, quite frankly, my perception of reality was violated on several occasions. But what I was left with more often than not was a deep sense of gratitude at what they were orchestrating on our (Humanity's) behalf. I was also deeply impressed by the vibrational quality of each of them. After listening, I was almost always left with deeply coherent emotions—feelings like love, gratitude, and a deep sense of inner peace and healing. On every occasion after recording them, I was touched and moved by the upliftment and the power that was communicated through their voices.

But it also became clear to me that their high spiritual vibrations were having a catalytic effect on me as well. One of the principles of vibrational healing is that a higher vibration will either drive out or transform a lower vibration. Thus, after listening to the recordings of these beings, I would often become aware of my own lower thought forms (meaning thought forms that limit freedom of expression and evolution).

Sometimes I would actually recall incidents from my past that were responsible for these thoughts and beliefs, while other times I simply felt them leaving me without any content or memory.

Thus, I have come to think of this recording as a potent form of spiritual purification. And that may actually be the main source of its power.

Through their singing to us, these spirit healers have managed to bring spiritual light into audible sound. And these sounds act as a kind of spiritual transformer. They draw out mental, emotional, and spiritual negativity (toxicity) and create a space within us for our own innate spiritual light to anchor more deeply and to manifest more clearly.

Through this process, I believe, our inherent self-healing abilities may also be enhanced.

Reading the article (which I did find pretty incredible) and listening to the music were two different experiences. Imagining (seeing) all these beings as they would send their sound healing through you was a pretty amazing experience by itself, and I think my readership enjoyed greatly reading it. I wanted them to read how an inter-dimensional music CD can be elaborated.

How can all these different sounds give a coherent sound at the end? We go from the Hathors, to the energy of Tao, to an African shaman with his medicine herbs and many others. For an untrained ear, the sounds seem similar at the end. How do you go about receiving all these different sounds and put out what seems "one" sound?

If you heard all the different thirty-two tracks playing at equal volume simultaneously, you would hear a cacophony of discordant sound.

When I mixed it, however, I brought out the inherent coherency, which took tens of hours of listening and premixing to find the right balance of the tracks.

Although I didn't mention it in the article, one interesting incident occurred about halfway through the recording process. The dominant voices were very highly catalytic, and people listening to the recording would have intense reactions and purification. It was only when the more calming and less catalytic voices were added that one could listen to it without so much reaction.

All the voices are present in the recording, but some are more dominant than others. The combination of all the voices affects the energetics of the recording even if some of them are more in the background.

Thank you.

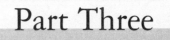

Part Three

THE HIGH COUNCIL
OF SIRIUS

INTRODUCTION FROM PATRICIA CORI

Just over ten years ago, I laid down in a crop circle and lost consciousness for over two hours. When I came back into my body, I was a changed woman—having been "rewired" to receive thought formations from a brilliant team of light beings who identified themselves to me as "Speakers of the Sirian High Council." They have come through the written word, they have spoken to us in the crops, and they have gone on to meet us, on many levels, in this exciting age of our starseed awakening. I thank them, yet again, for their unconditional love and compassion, helping us to understand the nature of the Cosmos and the limitlessness of all Creation.

Considering that I have always been quite discerning with regard to channelers and mediums and the source of their insights, I found it to be prophetic, in a sense, that I would be faced with the reality of serving in that same way—a vehicle through which the messages of extradimensional beings concerned with our evolution and planetary dynamics could be shared with the world.

As the voice of the Sirian High Council, it has been an incredible journey, bringing their wisdom and compassion to a growing global audience of countless starseed and spiritual seekers like you, who are preparing to help lead the way out of the restrictive thought programs that have for so long limited our perception of our true status as galactic beings.

Their works, *The Sirian Revelations*, have shown us the chains that have bound us to fear and resignation, just as they have shown us the keys to our liberation. They are the

"right now" of our experience, as we pass through the cor-
ridors of our transition, preparing to enter the bright light
of Arrival.

We are activating our energy networks, both within and
beyond our physical selves. We are reassembling the parts
that have gone lost, forgotten, scattered, and, above all, we
are remembering who we are and why we are here. In doing
so, we take responsibility for the world we have created and
recognize that we have *chosen* to be here. That is the key: It
is our choice to experience this! From that free will decision, we can only conclude the obvious: It serves us, at the
soul level, to experience all that is occurring in this time of
uncertainty and anticipation. Fully conscious, fully prepared
for all that evolves in these days of immense transition, we
are empowered when we understand the free will zone of
creative manifestation.

Once we surmount the rising fear, stimulated within us
by those who would hold us in servitude, we recognize that
we stand before Humankind's greatest hour: our reunion with
the galactic family, our true ancestors, and the imminent giant leap in the evolution of all life on our planet. Despite
the darkness of this, our hour of deliverance, we are ready to
be birthed in the light of a new dawn, and that is the most
remarkable of all our expectations.

Asked to share in creating this work of prophecy of what
lies ahead, I am honored to bring the vision and teachings of
the Council to you from the holy city of Abydos, in Egypt,
where I am discovering remarkable new insights into ancient
secrets. These I will soon elaborate in my upcoming work,

Where Pharaohs Dwell, which will tie together so many loose ends of the story of Atlantis and the Atlanteans' journeys to distant shores.

As we move ever closer to the end date of the Mayan calendar (December 21, 2012), we find ourselves projecting more and more into the future. And yet, say the Council, the future is an illusion—a mere projection of our collective thoughts and experience. They call us to remember that we create it and that we participate in the playing out of all circumstance. Their overriding message is to remind us to be fearless, noble, and loving—taking care to raise the vibration of our own bodies and minds, so that we can shine our inner light out to the world that surrounds us.

As we all seek out the seers, read the prophecies, and ponder the future, let us never forget that our beloved Earth Mother, Gaia, is the product of her karma and that each of us plays a part in it. Our every thought, emotion, and action moves through her heart and her soul, and she plays it back to us, loud enough for us to hear and feel our group intention.

As we peek into the illusive future in this work, let us never forget that it is the today of our lifetimes that we can effect: We can raise the vibration, through the heart, making the world within and beyond a more luminous place. Let us honor that responsibility, committing to every day, every moment, and doing the very best we can to shine the love of the One Heart into the darkness—holding a lantern for those who are lost in fear and despair.

In the eloquent words of my beloved master guides, the Sirian High Council:

"Let us be fearless, like the lion; acute, as the eagle; and gentle, like the dove: never doubting our strength; never losing our way; never forgetting that we are the *Gaian vibration rising.*"

My thanks to Martine Vallée,
for welcoming me to this project
and for her commitment to bringing the wisdom of Alexandria
back from the bonfires of ignorance past.
My love surrounds you,
Patricia Cori
"Trydjya," Scribe to the Sirian High Council
www.sirianrevelations.net

FROM THE HIGH COUNCIL OF SIRIUS

Greetings, starseeds, it is with great pleasure that we communicate with you at this moment of your time/space. We, the speakers of the Sirian High Council, represent the consciousness of countless Sirians who are connecting with Earth from the ascended star system of Satais or Sirius B. We are old, much older than you, and we know much about the Human race, for our elders were part of the Great Experiment—the seeding of your race.

At key times in your development, we have materialized on the Earth plane, crystallizing in matter so as to better serve Humankind—starseed of the Universe. This took place at the time of the second cycle of Atlantis, when you were blossoming in the light of that civilization; it occurred in ancient Egypt, and it is about to occur again, at the closing of the Mayan calendar.

We have come to serve you at this time of your evolution into the light body, for we know what awaits you—we have known your process. Many are the light beings now focused on Earth's transition; consciousness from the Pleiades and Andromeda are some of those working with you and joining us to help raise the vibration.

So let us begin our intervention by saying that all conscious beings in the Cosmos of Soul journey the spiral of darkness to light. Sparks of the infinite light, we first separate from Prime Creator, then leap into the abyss of darkness, to know the magnitude of all that is encompassed in the mind of God. Once we lose our fascination with the mysteries of shadow land, we proceed to climb the spiral of "I am" experience, to finally reach full illumination and return, to merge again into the absolute of a Oneness with all Creation: the Atum, the atom—the All That Is.

So it is for all the biological "units" living on your planetary home; so it is for every sentient being in the universe, as it is at every other station in the Cosmos, where life, in some form or another, flourishes. It is found in the density of the mineral realms, where molecular units of consciousness move so slowly as to *appear* not to be consciousness manifest—yet conscious they are indeed. It thrives in the animal kingdoms of the earth, sea, and skies, and finally to the species of *Homo sapiens*, the highest form of intelligent life in your world. It abounds in the microsphere, of which you have very limited awareness. Despite the countless forms and aspects, all with their different paces and rhythms (for this is the nature of the music of existence), all life is part of the same musical crescendo, eventually moving from darkness to light in all its manifestations.

As sparks of consciousness exploding, we are like embers from a fire, shooting out from the blazing flames and then, in turn, igniting and burning back into the one fire, as they are drawn back to their source . . . to merge there. In essence, we spend an eternity remembering that where we are headed is where we are from and that is the ultimate experience. That, starseed, is what we have come to learn; that is what we have come to remember.

That godliness within us all is forgotten when we take that bold leap into the densest of matter, separating (in a sense) from Source and plunging deep into the abyss. We become distracted by our own illusion, the fields of opposition, darkness and light—for exploring the artwork of the Creator, in all its shades and complexities, is what gives us a reason to exist as free-willed, individual units of the great light of Spirit.

In the journey of self-discovery, we spend much time in and give untold energy to the physical realm in which you currently find yourselves—the third dimension. There, after our emergence from the seemingly godless night, each of us is presented with choice: the opportunity to crawl, walk, or leap through the fields of illusion. We weigh each experience of darkness and light, the duality of the lower realms, and decide, of free will, how long we wish to linger in the shadow, but knowing, at the absolute soul essence level, that eventually all moves up the spiral. Everything—every conscious thought, every living being—eventually moves into the light.

We are assisted, in this journey, by those who have preceded us. They leave their markers, their teachings, to help us climb the stairways to the heavens . . . the pathway of return.

These works are often the gifts of highly evolved beings who leave testimonies to the question and search for an understanding of their own immortality, as is in the case of the high civilizations of many ancestral worlds of Gaia.

Know that we have worked with the vehicle, Trydjya (Patricia Cori), since her appearance in body in the middle cycle of Atlantis, where she served as a Keeper of the Crystals. Like many of you, she returned to physical form during the last generation of the Atlantean civilization, a karmic debt that has brought you, children of Atlantis, back to serve at this time. Under our tutelage, our channel. Trydjya has taken herself to the Holy of Holies, the Osireion, in the land of Khemit (Egypt), as part of her pursuit of that light. There will be challenges in her mission, for true initiations—the great leaps—are often fraught with obstruction . . . and many tests.

We are capable of reaching resonance with her as she attunes to those very powerful vibrational levels and as she experiences those frequencies shift within her. It is, in many respects, a different density—much lighter, much clearer—than that which we are used to in the city where she resides (Rome), and a much higher vibration is enjoyed by all as we open communication. It is a portal between life and death, matter and spirit—a gateway to the Halls of Amenti.

As our mind collective dances upon the light beams of ancient imprints, the worship of the gods, we celebrate with her. We feel her wonder, as she walks the halls of the pharaohs' idols, the gods of the Pantheon at Abdu (Abydos). Knowing the great works of which Humankind is capable, we gaze on the renaissance of your fallen ancestors, carved into the walls, just as they are etched into the ethos and imprinted in your collective unconsciousness. And we feel her adrenaline rising, as she peers into the dark tunnels of history to find the truths that lie waiting for her there.

Many of you resonate to these fields of consciousness, where light bearers of ancient Atlantis rebuilt the archetypal civilizations of those fallen lands. We understand your thirst to know more, now that Atlantis is rising in your memories and collective experience. And we remember, for there the Sirian imprint also rests, immortalizing the passing of our Elders. We have guided our channel to the Holy of Holies to reveal, from a Sirian perspective, its significance on your shifting reality at this hour of Human evolution. From that very sacred place, we welcome your quest to bring forward our visions of that point on the time-space continuum that we will identify as 2009.

Like a light flashing on a marquis, that location on the time-space continuum is the point of reference with which you will mark the most significant surges in the crescendo of celestial energies preparing for stellar ascension. Gaia, your great mother, will shake you from your comfort zones as you have never been shaken before. Ra, your sun, will blast you with the most incredible energy storms, within and beyond the atmosphere, with challenging moments for you all.

The pervading consciousness of materialism will be diminished, and, as difficult as it will be for many to let go of possession and need, there will be a growing return to the simplicity of exchange and sharing. 2009 will be a year of manifestation, as you prepare for the Age of Spirit. Will you fight to hold onto what you feel is yours, or will you let go and let God?

However difficult your decisions, however effortless, your soul is guided. You will find your way. Whether kicking and screaming, or whether running toward the unknown, trusting, you face the new unafraid, curious, ready.

You are blessed, starseed, to be living in this moment of revelation. We embrace you in the light of all that is shared on the spiral of limitless being, where each is All, and All is One.

We are the Sirian High Council.

Nineteen

THE MYSTERY OF EGYPT

Before going into the purpose of Patricia's mission today in Egypt, I would like, for the benefit of my readers, to discuss some aspect of Egypt that remains a mystery. Many of us who are living today had a life or many lives in this land after the sinking of Atlantis.

From my understanding, ancient Egypt seems almost to be a planet by itself. It seem to have developed at an extraordinary rate compared with others of the same time period. Not surprising, since its population were survivors of Atlantis. They seem to be the most extensive organized society at that period and well in advance in many aspects to other civilizations of that time.

Since the end of Atlantis was known well in advance, knowing your involvement in Egypt's history, was it decided on the part of the Sirian High Councils to simply concentrate or continue the knowledge of Atlantis in one place on Earth because of what was going to happen in the future?

We remind you that every soul of every realm of consciousness exists as master of its own destiny at the individual level, and as a vibrationally attuned co-creator of the collective experience. As Earth residents of the third dimension, you are co-creators of the Earth experience. Earth, in turn, co-creates the experience of your stellar being, Ra, of which it is, yet again, an aspect and a reflection.

We, intelligence of higher dimensions, focus on the events playing out in our realities, which are inevitably the result of those souls who have evolved to this point on the spiral of consciousness along with us. However, as All is One in the Cosmos of Soul, the consciousness of every level, every individual, every dimension is a reflection of the Whole, and therefore we are both affected by your reality and effective in it as well.

It is neither our desire nor our responsibility to decide what is to happen in the playing out of events in your realm, for that would be an act of altering your karmic process, as well as our own.

Rather, we have served at various intervals in certain evolutionary fields in order that we might shine more light down into the spiral, where those who climb from the various degrees of darkness and shadow lands are enabled to see more clearly what lies ahead—where the light becomes brighter with every step.

As to the question of Atlantis, we ask that you consider that the knowledge of that ancient world was not limited to the lands of the ancient Egypt—the Khemit. Rather, it was spread to many locations on the Earth, for the continent of Atlantis reached from its northern shores, icy and cold, to its southernmost tip, far below the steamy equatorial regions, and so enjoyed access and contact with indigenous populations of every imaginable description and place.

We believe that you are realizing this now, as you are discovering Atlantean philosophies, constructs, magic, and astronomical alignments in almost every continent of your modern world. You are discovering the recurring themes in the ancient stories. Much is coming to light now about your true origins, your true DNA coding, and soon the secrets of Atlantis—and all that occurred there—will be revealed as well. The Hall of Records beneath the Great Sphinx has already been located—but it has yet to be activated. Another secret chamber lies within the pyramid itself—this, too, has been discovered but has yet to reveal its purpose, for those who currently hold the keys to the gates are not of the light, and they come to the experience without love. They dig madly in the solar fields of the Giza energy complex, unable to put the pieces together, for fragments of their own souls are scattered like shards on the sands of time.

We tell you, do not fear or create dark illusions in your minds. Master Lightworkers of your great planet will be enabled to activate Giza and all the other Atlantean power stations when it is time to activate the Halls. For those of you wondering if we really said, "Master Lightworkers of your great planet will activate Giza . . . ," yes, we did. Very evolved Human Beings *are* light beings. There are many among you now, and many more are going to achieve illumination at the time of the Great Shift—and they will be guided by the Ascended Masters, some of whom you are aware of, and others have yet to rise in your conscious awareness.

As the sands of time have hidden, so have they revealed, awaiting the right coordinates on the time-space continuum. All is in perfect order as you approach the point of your acceleration out of the density and into the light. The thirteen Atlantean crystal skulls will be reunited at that time. The mindlight generators of Atlantis will illuminate the passageways. The Halls of Amenti will materialize before your eyes. This, all of this, will occur in your lifetimes.

We ask you to always bear in mind that much of this monumental wisdom, knowledge, and technology of the Atlantean experience was light filled, while some was very dark in its intent—

for throughout the millennia of Atlantis there were continuous cycles of darkness and light—in their ultimate intensity—and one of those cycles of extremes is now playing out in your contemporary Earth experience: the Desert Days.

Of this emergent Atlantean record, none remains more indelibly coded and secreted than in Egypt, where the records of your planet's experience are safely stored and encoded, and so much has survived the ravages and destruction of time, the shifting of the Earth's sands, and the Human hand. There lie so many buried secrets, disguised in the myths of the gods, which evolve from the early times of the third cycle of Atlantis—when Osiris (of Sirius) and his Atlantean queen Isis reigned in the resurrected lands of that great land.

This we will soon be revealed to you, knowing there will be controversy and resistance. Be aware of what it will evoke in those who cling to the belief systems of contemporary thought and declared expert historians.

At the time of the final catastrophe of Atlantis, over ten thousand years before the Christed One walked the Earth and twenty thousand years after their ancestors had burned the path, significant other numbers of the White Brotherhood escaped the catastrophe at the surface through the intricate tunnel networks and cities of inner Earth.

Some resurfaced in the lands of Khemit, where it was divined that there would be created all the record halls needed for the survival of the Atlantean record and, perhaps, the very Human race itself. Others fled to the Mayalands, the high grounds of Tibet and Peru, all with a mission to preserve the light of the Ancient Sun.

Dark Ones followed, for we remind you yet again that there is always darkness and light in the density of the third dimension. It is the nature of your reality. What you do with these vibrations, both as individuals and as a collective, is what determines the *future* as you know it, and that is not the work or the responsibility of those beyond your realm—although we do what we can to assist in your passage out of the darkness and into the light. We, too, have passed there. We, too, were aided by those further along, and so it goes.

Bearing in mind that your purpose along the journey is just as much to extend a hand to those who trail as it is to reach to the light one just ahead, you learn the true significance of lightworking for the greatest good of all.

We ask you always to remember as well that the future (as you know it) is never predetermined and that all is forever changing in the illusory world in which you dwell.

The past is an illusion—for it is a swirling canvas of memory in movement—and it is different for every single one of you.

The future is an illusion—for it is mere conjecture and is of the one and the many, malleable, changing with every karmic act. And the present, illusive, flees from your mind just as quickly as it comes into being.

Was Egypt a land of immortality and planned that way?

We will answer your question from different perspectives to cover all aspects of it. We will begin by saying that predynastic Egypt was a time of pure Atlantean and Sirian influence on the receptive indigenous tribes of the Khemit, where the history of

Atlantean existence and evolution was brought to manifestation. Through the use of sound, conscious thought, and light,
the spiritual indigenous people were shown the wonders of far
more ancient days, while the wonders of their own were inte-
grated into a new form—the Egyptian High Culture.

These works, pre- and post-Atlantean Khemitian records,
are very much a part of the great works of your Egyptian ancestors, and they are intertwined throughout the myths. What was
"planned" for Humanity was of a twofold purpose:

• To immortalize the record of all that came *before* (symbolized by the left eye of Horus)

• To serve to awaken and activate that consciousness for
what laid ahead of you (symbolized by the right).

Despite attempts by historians to conceal the truth of the
Atlantean legacy, you no doubt have gleaned from all that has
been left for you that the immensity of Egypt's High Culture,
with its profound knowledge and technology, does not fit the
"time line" of the archeological record. We speak of that con-
struct on the space-time continuum that marked the "end" of the
third cycle of Atlantis and the "beginning" of the high society
of Egypt, which declined, in focus and spirit, with each new
dynasty—as the land of ancient Egypt.

However, we ask you to bear in mind that traces of the Great
Civilization of Atlantis—at the time when Osiris walked—still
exist in Egypt and that it is the memory and discovery of the
Osiris cult that mark the intervention of the Great Atlanteans
in Khemit.

That generation of Atlanteans, you are soon to discover, was
far more important than the last, and it is their contribution

that is most important to you now. It is best to clarify that by "land of immortality" we understand your question to mean that you wish to know if it was intended that Egypt serve as the storehouse of the Atlantean wisdom from which it sprang forth and flourished. We confirm to you that it has indeed been constructed so that the secrets of Humanity's passing through the greatest hours of its existence on the Earth plane would remain safeguarded, until such time as the Human race would reach the level of understanding to decipher the coded wisdom, activate the keys of multidimensional experience, and utilize it all for the highest good of Gaia and worlds beyond.

Through its unlimited archeological record and rich mythological legends, Egypt reveals to the Initiate the spiritual mastery and wisdom of the highest societies of ancient Atlantis, just as it holds the keys to the story of the last generations. It is all there for you, immortalized in stone and in the unspoken word, for you to peer into as a living tapestry of what you believe is past— and to unravel and activate—as a gateway to the new dawn. A more perfect reflection of its immortality cannot be found!

This is our understanding of your question regarding the intention that Egypt be an immortal land, for in continuing the legacy of Atlantis and projecting it into your contemporary consciousness, it has indeed rendered Atlantis and its people immortal in your experience.

If, instead, your question was intended to mean a "land of immortality" where the focus of life was preparation for the eternal life of the soul, with the resurrection of the physical being— let us say to you . . . yes, the quest for immortality of the soul and the resurrection of the physical being were the quintessential focus of life in ancient Egypt. From the myths of the "first time" or Zep Tepi, as described in Egyptian texts, early religious cults of Egypt taught that like Osiris, the individual could achieve immortality and retain physical presence in the afterlife. This quest for life eternal, misinterpreted from the earliest stories of Osiris and his otherworldly presence so many millennia prior, was unquestionably an overriding theme in the evolution of Egyptian culture. What remains today, in the evidence brought forward from the tombs of old, are symbols of the Egyptians' search to achieve immortality, obtained through three distinct processes. The first was the mummification of the body, painstakingly undertaken to preserve the physical form. The second was to provide all the essentials that would be required by the spirit on its passing: nourishment, tools, and personal items of significance to the departing one. The third required incantations and magical spells that remained buried with the body so that the spirit could rise from the body and journey to the Halls of Amenti.

The pursuit of eternal life is a recurring theme throughout the Human experience for it is you remembering, at the primordial level, that the disempowering idea of finality—your death—is only an illusion and that the soul is eternal.

What was the specific role of the Sirians at the time of Osiris, Isis, and Horus?

The question of our presence at this point of the story of Atlantis/ Egypt is complex and one that requires significant elaboration— which we are preparing to do with our channel in the upcoming work, *Where Pharaohs Dwell*, evolving from her time at the Holy of Holies. There are many layers, many aspects to the story, and so many clues have been left for you—almost all of which have been misinterpreted by historians. Often in your search for answers regarding your multidimensional existence, you overlook the fact that the illuminated masters among you have shown you the art of materializing, dematerializing, and rearranging the Atum to create new forms. You ask yourselves, "Did gods truly descend from the heavens to walk amongst us?" and ponder their intervention, as well as ours, in your worlds.

In the case of the Osiris legend, it is one and the same. Osiris (anagram of Sirios) was a master of light from the Sirian star system who made his entry into your world through a portal created early on, at the beginning of the third cycle of Atlantis. We have elaborated this information in our prior work, *Atlantis Rising*, describing how beings of Yzhnüni, a Sirian satellite, retrograded into your dimension to serve in the evolution of the Atlanteans:

We reiterate that the third and final cycle of Atlantis began with the melting of the ice sheets. As the glaciers began their rapid retreat from the continent, a great flourishing occurred rather spontaneously and Atlantis, one of the last land masses to experience the devastation, was one of the first to be revitalized . . . both energetically and climatically. Many Sirian souls chose to incarnate upon the Earth at that time to assist in the rebirthing of the Human race as part of our karmic bond with you, and to settle our unresolved karmic issues with the Annunaki of Nebiru. We were able to read the Akashic

Record and observed that the Family of Light would be called into Earth's fields at that time, and so it was believed, in a sense, to be our destiny to incarnate below our vibration in a return to the third dimension.

This was a time when the first Sirians appeared as Humanoids upon the face of the Earth, specifically in the mountain lands of Atlantis. Like our Solar Deity, Satais (Sirius B), the planet body of their origin, Yzhnü, is no longer of the material universe, for it resonates at a higher frequency—a six-dimensional planetary essence which exists in a parallel universe alongside yours.

For the Yzhnüni, it was a chance to live again in form, with all the challenges consciously evolving beings would face from the elements, the other life forms and the transmutational process of retrogradation, while resolving the karma that, binding Sirius to the Gaian vibration, would have forever delayed our own evolution. The Yzhnüni, starseed of Sirius, experienced great difficulty crystallizing in the third dimension, for theirs was a vibration which had long before passed from physicality and the return to material form was riddled with uncertainly. Yet, reports of the blue-green planet, her majesty and music, sang through the universe and her fascination was immense.

Quite simply, Gaia was the siren of the heavens and these Sirian souls were the Ulysses of the galactic seas. Their essence crystallized in the three-dimensional fields of earth reality as very tall, radiant hominids, of a form that closely resembled Human anatomy and structure . . . but which clearly was not. Most distinguishing were their extensive auric fields, which emanated visibly many feet beyond their physical bodies. Their outer coverings were like a delicate foil, absolutely white and translucent, so that to the natives they appeared as fairy-like beings and were perceived as such for many centuries of their existence in the earth sphere. They had enormous, bright eyes, which reflected the color indigo; their hair was of the golden white light; their eight-foot tall bodies were slender, delicate and lithe. The Yzhnüni resonated most closely to the earth element of water, of their planet was abundant in it, as are the other natural satellites in the Sirian system. In order to hold the Gaian frequency, they were germinated in the highlands of the continent of Atlantis, for there were innumerable caves and grottoes in which they could find the warmth and moisture that best replicated their natural environment, while protecting them from the radiation emitted by the powerful rays of your Solar Deity. It was a terrain that most closely typified the crystalline fields of Yzhnü.

With their first appearance upon the Earth, the Yzhnüni were of such a high vibratory frequency that they could not hold form in the density of your planetary field, nor could they bear any contact with the direct rays emanating from the Sun. To observers, they would have appeared to fade in and out of reality, and they did, indeed, bleed out of the world of matter and back into the sixth dimension repeatedly, until they were finally capable of holding 3D frequency. Their outer sheaths contained none of the pigment required to protect them from the damaging ultraviolet light, and so they were underground in the sunlight hours during those early days of their "distant" migration.

In time, as this Sirian seed took root in three-dimensional reality, their physical beings became denser and more adapted to Earth's geothermal forces and its relationship to the Sun, which once again shone brilliantly through Earth's atmosphere. Their bodies became more solid and resilient, their skin became more opaque and their coloring took on slightly deeper hues . . . a somewhat less translucent quality.

This portal was a gift from Sirius to the Atlanteans and to all generations of Humankind to come, to be utilized at those enormously pivotal times in accelerating Human consciousness when the stargates could be opened. Such a time occurred then, when Osiris descended through the gateway from the higher dimensions and into the third, and another occurs in short order, when you reach the ascension vortex. Again, we talk about this in *Atlantis Rising:*

> At a point in the Yzhnüni's earthly evolution, during which time they had effectively trained the novitiates in those practices that would help re-establish the warm frequencies of the natives and the entire ecosystem, the Sirian High Council intervened. We were intent upon accelerating the Atlanteans' understanding of multidimensionality and the higher purpose of Humankind's

existence, so that they would be able to carry on with the Yzhnüni's work of jump-starting the civilization's collective memory. It would connect them with the infinity of life streaming through the multidimensional body of All-That-Is.

It was our intention to ensure that the Yzhnüni's presence amongst your great ancestors serve to elevate the mutating starseeded Human race from the bondage of survival mind into the pursuit of enlightenment, and to teach the Wisdom to those who would guide the people in that quest. We were directed to help dissolve the grid that had been made to envelop the Earth, so that we could re-establish direct lines of contact with you and with other life forms of your world.

To assist the noble Yzhnüni in their efforts, thirteen crystal skulls of extra-dimensional origins were brought into materialization, "crystallized" in three-dimensional earth frequencies much as you, as soul essences create the physical bodies in which you reside as 3D beings. Remember that quartz crystals are living beings, which record, store and amplify energy. You have seen this in their practical application in your technology and, although you may not quite understand how it works, you have accepted the use of the silicon chip as the foundation upon which that very technology is built. Never forget, however, that throughout the universe of matter and permeating the infinite dimensions beyond your current "slice" of reality, the capacity of crystal beings to serve consciousness is exalted when the matrix is activated by directed, focused thought waves of the few and the many. When that focus is set for the highest possible good of the All, magic happens.

As difficult as it might be for you to visualize or to accept, it is quite a simple process bringing crystal beings from an etheric imprint into matter, and this you may have already witnessed in your personal interactions with them. You may have experienced a crystal simply disappearing and then returning to you at another time or place. This is a phenomenon of universal scope and frequency and no, you aren't losing your mind if one of your crystal teachers seems to "disappear into thin air." It is just that the illusions of the world of matter may have you believing that such things cannot happen, just as you may believe that you, too, cannot disappear and return at will. Yet, such occurrences are reported frequently in those lands of ascetics and masters who achieve dematerialization as a result of what you term "mind over matter." The thirteen skulls brought into manifestation in early Atlantis were "sculpted" as a result of the mind-patterning of higher beings—members of the Family of Light—who were called from many dimensional frameworks to participate in their creation. Delivered unto the earth realm by the Sirian High Council, they were programmed to open the portals of multidimensional awareness to the Yzhnüni . . . that they could continue their work with direct access to guidance from the higher dimensions. The thirteen skulls, known to the Family of Light as "The Skull Committee," were stationed in the Temple of Nephthys, deep within an

amethyst grotto in the inner earth sanctuary of Yzhnüni
worship.
—from *Atlantis Rising*

Osiris, Master of the Golden White Light, came to Earth through
the portal opened with the Skull Committee to draw the survivors of second-cycle Atlantis out of their sanctuaries within the
Earth, so that they might rebuild your world.

A master of light over matter, he was worshipped as the
quintessential god of Egypt from which all other records and
mythologies spring. We have much more to share with you, as
is appropriate to your discoveries now, of Osiris and the significance of the thirteen skulls of Atlantis.

What is your role today?

We understand your question to be in reference to our interac-
tion with Earth beings at this point on the time-space continuum, whose vibration is rising in harmony with the mutating
frequencies of your solar deity, as he prepares for ascension.

As in other pivotal moments in Human evolution, wherein
your species enjoyed incredible leaps of individual and so-
cietal advancement, you are all at the point of reconnection
with the Galactic Family. This involves, among many other
things, the arrival of significant numbers of extraterrestrial,
three-dimensional beings (from within and beyond your solar
system), as well as contact from intelligent extradimensional
light beings from the higher dimensions.

Some of the extraterrestrials in question will be of the lower vibrations; some will be of the higher. This is the nature of the duality of physical reality, as we have described to you so many times in our works. Some are already well established on the Earth, involved with your governments and their agendas, as we have described to you previously; others are soon to arrive. Some are of the dark persuasion, some of the light; others are somewhere in between.

As to the question of their intention for the interspecies development that will evolve from their interactions with the Human race, we remind you that it is the energetic fields of your creative individual and collective thought patterns that will determine how you will receive alien contact, which will, in turn, determine their natural reactions to you. The responsibility of the light realms in which we hold resonance is to rekindle within you the knowledge of how you co-create reality with every thought, every word, and every action, serving as a station in mind-space whereby you can receive love and light and dispel fear.

That is our true purpose in making contact with you now, as it has always been across the fields of probability, which you know as the time-space continuum.

This, dear starseed, has been eloquently represented in the pantheon of Egyptian gods, through which your ancestors sought wisdom, guidance, and light from the beyond. Like the ancients, you strive to know what lies beyond the realm of the physical and all that is manifest within your fields of observation.

And, like the Egyptians and other ancient starseed, you are being facilitated to receive the knowledge firsthand, as you evolve with the rising vibrations of Earth.

Was the Great Sphinx a testimony to the beginning of a new era? I ask because I see that usually for a long time the vision of the gods was depicted as a Human body with an animal head—and then the sphinx is an animal body with a Human head. What was the reason for this?

The Great Sphinx, a Sirian effigy, was not originally created with a Human head—this transformation was undertaken millennia after its creation, and it was a deliberate act intended to feed the ego of the pharaoh and, in so doing, break the energy.

Even casual observation will reveal to you that the current Humanlike head is utterly but of proportion with the leonine body, which stares out to the east, across the horizon, at the Sirian star of Sothis.

The Lioness bears witness to ancient starseed, those of early days in the third cycle of Atlantis, who worshipped the sister stars from that point on Gaia's power grid that corresponded with the epicenter of her energy body and the merging of all ley lines within and upon the surface of your planet. She is the guardian of the fields, holder of the musical scores of Giza that, once revealed, will activate the Hall of Records.

I have to ask: What is beneath the Sphinx? We hear for so long about so many different things.

Beneath the Lioness lies the Hall of Records in which are recorded all the thoughts ever thought, all the words ever spoken, and every sacred code ever encoded in the multidimensional universe.

There are found all the keys to activate the network of pyramids on all continents, the temples of all worshippers, the energy grids of the outer and inner bodies of Gaia, and access routes to Agartha.

There lies an unadorned chamber, circular in form (representative of the Atum, the One of Creation), that serves as a resonance chamber for the music of creation to be played when the time is reached that Human consciousness can decipher just how the symphony is written and stored in the Sphinx.

Your archeologists have already penetrated this sacred space, disappointed at its simplicity and barren walls, for they have no idea of its purpose. Spiritual masters will be enabled to decode the many layers of consciousness and sound the music, and that will only occur when the Human race has made the shift, creating the necessary harmonics.

Is what is under the Sphinx related to Giza?

Yes, it is all interrelated, most certainly. We confirm to you that the Great Pyramid serves many purposes, among which it is a chariot in which the pharaohs enjoyed time travel. From the so-called sarcophagus in the king's chamber, they journeyed to many star systems and many dimensions.

Following the principles of simple harmonic motion, wherein multiple frequencies are symmetrical to one point, creating resonance fields, the entire plateau was in harmonic, meaning in proportion to the chamber beneath the Sphinx.

All that is visible to the Human eye (the structures that stand above the sands) and all that lies hidden to all but the elite who secretly explore the below there and at other strategic locations are harmonically tuned to specific frequencies and musical sequences that can be "played," in a sense, to open the Hall of Records.

It is a slightly oval-shaped space, in the underground, baffling the archeologists, for it holds no apparent treasure, bears no inscription, and reveals nothing of its wisdom of Humankind's birth and history. All is coded, awaiting the direction of the maestro who can orchestrate the great symphony that will turn the keys.

There are tunnels all through and below in the area known as the Giza Plateau. These multileveled passageways connect the Pyramids, the Sphinx, underground cities in their entirety, and burial grounds still rich in history and the material wealth sought out by your modern-day conquistadores.

The main passageway, a sacred path into the heart of the Hall of Records, is located between the arms of the Sphinx—just there, behind the breastplate. There only the initiated can pass through the multidimensional doorway, for no physical manifestation exists.

Twenty

THE ALEXANDRIAN LIBRARY AND THE VATICAN

A while ago, information was given to me that, in a past life, I was one of the keepers of the Alexandrian Library. The vision that I seem to have of this is that I see myself an old man, lying on the floor, dying of grief from guilt of not being able to save the great knowledge contained in this place. In my soul, I believed that it was the beginning of a very dark period for Humanity because without that knowledge, everything would become limitless.

At that time, there were many great libraries throughout the world. The Alexandrian Library was situated on a seaport. It seems to carry a very special energy that had nothing to do with our Earth plane. In fact, it came from outside light forces. It has been said that some documents from the Alexandrian Library were copied or saved and sent in different places on Earth. One of those places is the Vatican. When I research this, I've learned that there are over two hundred vaults of archives, and each archive may have over two hundred thousand documents.

Since knowledge is freedom, was the burning of this library a plan from the dark forces to take away all knowledge?

First, let us tell you that, yes, upon gazing the screen of the no-time, we see your hands burned in the flames of the great halls of learning. You did suffer there and continue to suffer the memory of that incredibly dark act against Humankind. But contrary to your belief and the statement above, when the library burned, the works were, to a very great extent, relieved of their limitations and purified in the flame—to be imprinted, in a higher form, in the ethers.

Does the work that you are doing today have anything to do with this past life? Yes. You are here to bring back to the people the knowledge of their multidimensional consciousness. One of your missions in this moment of time/space is to continue the work with which you resonate in that field of consciousness in which *Alexandria* holds vibration, but you must heal the karma and release the pain.

Having said that, those of you reading this know that at any moment and at any point in the three-dimensional universe where there exists power structure or individuals whose intention it is to rule over any sentient beings or race, there will also exist a desire to withhold any form of knowledge and wisdom as a fundamental strategy of control. Domination over another is constructed not only of the whip and sword, for that is so overt in its manifestation that the sublimated can face and potentially overcome the tyrant. Instead, it is the manipulation of consciousness, whereby the individual or society is led away from the light of love and the wonders of universal mind (expressed so eloquently by the ancient luminaries) to wallow in the slowed vibrations of ignorance and darkness that ultimately serve as the key to control and dominate others.

This occurs throughout your history, as it does on other unevolved planets of your dimension, for it is an aspect of the dual nature of your reality. And it is cyclical. You build and burn, raise and level, design and destroy, and then re-create it all—over and over again. Do bear in mind and soul, however, that in the act of burning the books, what occurred was the imprinting of the wisdom on the ethers—where the visions and insights of such enlightened contributors to the Human story have been etched on the Akashic Record. This is the true library of Earth, and all is written, from the first thought of Atum, Prime Creator, across the infinite seas of the Cosmos, and from the first atom itself.

If this library was under the guidance of the light forces, then why was it permitted that so much of the history of Earth, teachings, and information be burned?

Everything is God, Prime Creator, the Seed Thought. All springs from that Divine Will, the Goodness, the Essence, the Source, and so it is that everything that occurs in the illusion in which you reside is a playing out of cause and effect, darkness to light . . . infinitely, eloquently, and with profound experience and wisdom rising from the dance of opposition and harmony.

There have been so many Dark Ages in your history. Atlantis, Lemuria, Alexandria, the Crusades, and even now, your contemporary Earth societies are at the destruction point, appearing to careen toward your own annihilation. You know, however, that, like the Phoenix, you always arise, resurrecting yourselves from the ignorance that drives you to the extremes: back in flight, toward the light. You call these periods "eras of rebirth," and with each you rise higher than the epoch that led you there.

We ask you to consider that, as such, the darkness of such moments and their violent acts (to which the collective nonetheless contributes through its passivity and materialism) are as much a part of the light that rebounds from the gloomy caves of the collective unconscious as is the brilliance of resurrection itself.

Can we retrieve this knowledge from the guidance realm?

Yes, indeed, you do have the capabilities now to retrieve all wisdom from the Akashic Record, for you are fast remembering that you are multidimensional beings, created in the mind of Prime Creator, a spark of the Eternal Light.

Much of the library of scrolls is so utterly antiquated that, given an opportunity to return to that place on the time-space continuum that preceded the burning, you might just find the anticipation far exceeded the experience.

We urge you to forgive the past injustices and to understand how they serve you and then concentrate your mind and heart on the very now of your existence, for you are alive in one of the most revealing of all eras of history: the Dawn.

Soon you will be able to read the scrolls of countless ancient sages and the holograms of those who appear beyond you in the matrix of Human experience, right there, from the comfort of your armchairs on eternity—activated to see what, for most, has been hidden.

You are passing out of the Dark Age of contemporary repression and ignorance, dear one, into the Light of the Forever Fields.

Will the Vatican ever release some of this information?

It is doubtful. With all its links to the secret societies and power brokers of the Earth, the power network that rules over you, it is designed to hold you in obedience. Why, then, would its rulers provide you with the knowledge that would release you from their hold over such a vast part of your contemporary societies, especially now—as they push forward the agenda of another of their so-called holy wars? "Holy war"? How irreverent an utterance!

No, indeed, as long as the power brokers remain on their gilded thrones, they will hold onto what they believe are theirs to hold from you: *The lost scrolls of enlightenment.*

They have raped the great libraries, defaced and hidden the codes, and putrefied the wells of pure vision, because they believe themselves (privileged members of the ruling elite) in every way superior to you, the "masses."

They believe that, as a body of beings to be controlled and made to serve, you are more easily restrained when you are herded into the corrals of ignorance and blind obedience. And so they cling hard and fast to those tattered pages of past masters, many of whom were true visionaries, working for the light, and others—who were not.

Let this not surprise you. Many of those intellectual masters of the past explored the mysteries of ancient worlds—their technologies, sciences, and records of galactic events—in order to manipulate form and vibration to alter the power grids of global rule. Of these, significant numbers were enslaved to the dark forces of control on your planet, and their intentions were of the lowest vibration. These secrets, elaborated by those of the dark intent, are being used today as they were then.

Others, the light bringers, were guided to help lift Humankind out of the deep valleys of repression and onto the mountaintops of illumination. And here again, the wisdom of those light ones of old era are being retrieved by those Lightworkers of your era who come to the information with the light intent and that focus is manifesting with the raising of Human consciousness. Remember, however, that we have told you in our works that you would first pass through the Desert Days on your way to the dawn, and that is where you are now.

Once you remember that the overriding experience of the reality in which you hold residence is the existence of duality at all levels, you will understand that every action does indeed hold an equal and opposite reaction and that, in the great scheme of things in the Cosmic Order, it all eventually reaches resolution.

When you have mastered simplicity of thought and mind, you will recognize that the great scholars devoted their lifetimes to exploring the wonders of Creation and the perfection of existence. Upon these observations they traveled the roads of intellect and contemplation to bring you their works. We invite you always to remember that their most complex observations are found everywhere in nature, and these same principles are there for you to uncover with your own eyes: the cosmometry of life, the form, the color, the vibration. All the wisdom that you believe "lost" lies before your very eyes, within reach: in the petals of a rose; as the colors of the sky across the spectrum of Earth's revolutions; from the magnificence of your own incredible form.

Is it an energy of fear?

We believe that ignorance and fear are interchangeable and that any time one soul intends power over another, it is essentially an act of ignorance of one's godliness (however dim the spark shines within), just as it is a manifestation of that same individual's fascination with the lowest sensory vibrations that come with the first leap into the abyss into which new souls leap from Source.

Inherent in the worship of darkness is the fear that one will never reach the light and that there is far more safety in controlling a loveless reality of false mastery and worship than there is in surrendering, egoless to the Light.

Will we have to wait until after 2012 for these vaults to be open?

Dear one, the vaults are opening! You are the turners of the pages of ancient texts once you understand that you contain all the wisdom of the Universe in every cell of your memory and that the Akashic Record lies just as much within you as it does in the ethers.

As you evolve into higher states of consciousness, you begin to pull this universal wisdom out of the waters of your ancestral wells—your subconscious—and into the stream of contemporary thought. Remember that all that was written was burned into the ethers: it is but a reflection of the All That Is, That Ever Was, and That Always Will Be.

Much of it you have already learned; some you are discovering has not been lost, such as the sculpted record; more is being healed at the etheric level so that it can progress into the higher realms and find the light of higher consciousness.

If there are archives in the Vatican, surely there are some elsewhere. Would there be some under the Pyramids? I heard that some were also in France, Tibet, under the sands of Baghdad—even in the United States there are some. Is that so?

These libraries are not only textual, you do understand. Wherever Humankind faced prosecution for free thought, it was most often necessary to bury the profound revelations in codes, much as the greatest written texts of your present awareness: the Torah, the Bible, and all books of ancient religions. All are coded.

Our own messages are coded with multiple layers of consciousness, energy, and vibration. This is not a difficult process to achieve when you have cracked the codes of multidimensional communication. These libraries you so mourn are often right in front of you—in great artworks, in architecture, in nature's own design. And, again we remind you that the books you so long for are merely interpretations of those essential universal properties of God, life, and your existence as both sparks of Creation and as units of self-awareness within those frameworks.

Trust us. The actual physical libraries of old have been outdated by the laboratories and universities of modern Earth societies just as they have been raised even further in conscious application within your spiritual circles of light and Gaia's radiant fields.

I read also that there are places in the Vatican where Humans cannot walk. What kind of energy is in that place to produce such a thing? If so what is the purpose of this energy? Are they afraid of what we would discover in these vaults?

Yes, this is true, but it is nothing more than an energy force field creating a shield of protection against entry into the secret vaults. It is similar to the Vril Power that guards the entry points into the inner world of Agharta, although it is far less complex than that which is needed to seal the tunnels into the sacred world that lies within Gaia.

The Vril force described in some of your earlier texts is created by the manipulation of gravitation forces to such an extent that, applied, they can disassemble the cellular makeup of any biological life form that happens into it.

This force, one of the oldest technologies of Humankind, has been harnessed by the power elite and is used in many applications on Earth and in space. Although they have yet to master it, they do know far more than you are privileged to, and much of this information has come from the texts of old, just as it has been gifted from aliens friendly with your governments.

Twenty-One

THE MISSION AND INITIATION IN EGYPT

PATRICIA CORI

Could you describe the work that you were called to do in Egypt in December 2007?

In these years since my first clear contact from the Sirian High Council, I (like so many of us) have been thrown about on the path of spirit, tested, challenged, and rewarded as the search for knowledge has guided me to the sacred sites of the Earth. There, as the Council explained to us, are encoded the teachings of the ancient sages, and these are most often located at the highest vibration vortices we find in power points of the planet.

In the case of this particular journey to Egypt, for which I was told I would be asked to connect into the absolute heart center of this land, Abydos, I have been guided to travel into the passageways below the great Osireion in order to receive the stores of galactic information that are encoded in the mineral realms below.

This message was given me by the Sirian High Council, who are guiding me to and through all the sacred sites and holy temples of this Earth in these very powerful years of my life—as a student of spirit and guide to others. There I was shown what I believe is one of the greatest secrets yet to be retrieved, and it is very exciting to bring it forward in these days of discovery, as it links so many things together and helps me understand, at a very personal level, what is happening now.

I make no claim of its importance to others, since it is such a subjective experience. I merely bring forward my own experience to be shared, trusting that it will serve the greater good. It will be elaborated in my work in progress—*Where Pharaohs Dwell*—which I hope to complete in the months ahead.

Below the magnificent Temple of Sety I in Abydos lies the Osireion, a megalithic structure that has yet to be understood by archeologists, for it truly doesn't seem to fit in any established time frame of dynastic Egypt. To date, no known researcher or Egyptologist has been able to identify its purpose, explain its design, or postulate its significance. It remains, for all intents and purposes, an enigma. It has been compared to the stone structure of the Temple of the Sun in Peru, for its strangely cut corner megalithic pillars, which appear in that civilization—but not in Egypt.

Although in the past it was possible to enter into the Osireion, today it is forbidden by the Department of Antiquities, given the fact that the entrance and inner rooms are swamped with stagnant, putrid waters too deep to wade through—or at least that is the reason given. From what I have seen in this experience, from both a physical experience and an astral journey into the depths of the structure, I believe we are about to discover one of the most important aspects of our past and future here.

What kind of ritual did you do in the Osireion?

As always, doors open for me in most miraculous ways. I was given the opportunity to spend private time in the grounds of the Osireion without a soul around me other than the true temple guardian, Amir, who held the space for me at all times during my ritual work in Osireion and in the glorious Temple of Sety I.

I am blessed to be the guardian of a magnificent Mayan crystalline skull, Estrella, which was gifted to me during a ritual in Palenque in 2005, during which time I brought a SoulQuest journeys group to the sacred sites of the Maya. Since receiving it from the Mayan shaman, Kayun, I have been guided to bring it with me to every ceremony, in every site, that I am conducting in these years of discovery and spiritual journeying. The most important of the rituals I performed in the Osireion was to place the crystal skull into the murky waters for purification. This was not an easy task, as the water is deep and the skull could easily have fallen out of reach, so I had to hold onto it while going into the altered state of consciousness.

Then, too, I had to overcome my own discomfort over the appearance of the water, which is a cesspool of pollution, waste, and slime, and raise my consciousness to understand that the water is sacred. I had to override the illusion of appearances and embrace the higher understanding of the waters, and this, of itself, was an aspect of the Initiation. I was guided that my feet and hands would have to be in the water as well, and this, too, I followed, with difficulty, knowing that the energies of this holy place would nonetheless hold the water sacred, despite the appearance it held.

I held Estrella in the waters of the Osireion, my feet dangling there as well. My physical sight clouded over, opening the way for third eye visions.

The skull began to speak, as she has on other occasions.

Beneath these waters lies a secret that you are invited to bring back to the world. Peer into the well, center yourself in humility, and fear not. You are surrounded in the Golden White Light of Osiris, Master of the light realms of Sirius.

Of the thirteen crystal skulls of Atlantis, which we have described to you as the "Skull Committee," the Master lies in the deep earth below this Temple: the burial place of the Osirian effigy—the gateway to the Halls of Amenti.

It is the thirteenth of those crystal skulls that were gifted to Humankind during the time of Atlantis that lies buried here, its etheric blueprint contained within a protective shield, where also is found the DNA of the Sirian Master, Osiris.

Look deep, starseed, deeper than you have ever looked before. Guided by the Councils of Sirian Light, you have been asked here to unveil the secrets and discover the true road to Amenti. You will have been initiated when you have brought our experience to the Mayalands—where preparations are being made to reunite the Atlantean skulls.

You will be challenged, obstructed, and deterred. It is not new to you; however, this will be your greatest challenge. This is the way of the Spirit Warrior. You move forward, egoless, in service to the All.

Always remember, starseed, your path is illuminated, and you know how to shield yourself from the dark force just as you know when to shine the light of truth into the shadows.

The journey of soul purification that followed that announcement, and my visions as I passed through the underworld or passageways below the Osireion, has been monumental for me, and I am still decoding the experience. Moreover, I am still working through the process, trying to decipher the meaning to my personal life and the significance, if any, that it holds for others. When that has come clear, I will write about it—this is certain.

What is the purpose of this initiation and how is it related to today?

In the process of passing tests and the endless initiations we undertake as souls moving into higher vibrations, we are not always privileged to know the purpose of every step we take on the long road of return. What I do glean from these very intense experiences is, on many levels, very personal. It requires much introspection to learn, as a student of spirit, what their purpose is to my soul's progression and how it all serves the highest good. We are asked to listen to the guidance, follow our hearts, and take the leaps of faith that often seem so insurmountable, dangerous, and devoid of logic. It requires letting go of the fear of judgment and criticism and, above all else, holding the ego at bay.

I have learned in my work with the Council to try, as best I can, to silence the left brain, the voice of logical thought, and follow the intuition to become as receptive as possible to energies, thought patterns, and vibrations as I can. This, then, I reflect back in every way possible, to those with whom I interact— either energetically or through the word. In the desire to remain in humility before the wondrous events that unfold around me, I can merely state that I have had a monumental experience. I know that it will be disregarded by many who deny anything other than the so-called scientific proof, but, nonetheless, I will move forward with the information that was given to me, and I will go to the Mayan shamans with the encoded skull, Estrella, trusting that it will be received with open hearts and minds.

We will need to wait to see what unfolds as we pass the time marker of December 21, 2012.

Nonetheless, I believe that the unification of the thirteen crystal skulls will be facilitated by our collective understanding of the meaning of the resurrection of Osiris (when the thirteen pieces are reunited to birth Horus) and that our ability to understand this metaphor will facilitate the activation of the crystal skulls. This is our collective experience, not a personal one. The joy is understanding how it all fits together and being egoless in whatever role I or anyone else will play in that moment. It is so important to be in surrender and service.

What will happen when the reunification takes place?

That wealth of information, the Earth Record, will be available to us all, and with the opening and merging of the gateways, we will be journeyers on the galactic highways. We will see the entirety of it all—the workings of the physical universe and beyond—and we will "realize the Atum."

What do you understand the Council to mean when they speak of realizing the Atum?

I understand this metaphor of the Council's to be telling us that the physical universe in which we reside is but a single atom—like Atum, lord of creation—and that it is merely a microcosmic speck on the infinity of all consciousness. Once we understand that, as sparks of the godlight, we are eternal, infinite, and unlimited, we will throw off the shackles of your limitation and reach illumination—realizing the Atum.

What drew you to Abydos?

This remote location in the deserts of the Sahara, the Holy City of Abydos, is believed to be the oldest known place of spiritual pilgrimage—older than Mecca, Jerusalem, or anyplace in between. From as long ago as predynastic times, this location has been recognized as the absolute spiritual epicenter of Egypt and believed, by many, to be the spiritual core of ancient days as far back as predynastic record. There is the magnificent Osireion, which I now believe is truly the resting place of the head of Osiris (as intended to mean the thirteenth crystal skull). It is the primary passageway into the Halls of Amenti. There are the burial grounds, soon to be excavated—these will make the current Valley of Kings look like a mere minimuseum. There are the villages, magical unto themselves, where ancient temples lie buried here and there, in the sands of time. And, of course, there is the splendid temple of Sety I of Abydos, the best preserved in the whole Egyptian realm. Here, the gods depicted in the walls and the energies they represent are alive—you can be transported and communicate with them. That, too, is part of a message I will soon share.

The temple of Abydos, a shrine built by the Pharaoh Sety I to the gods, is the ultimate temple to the gods. It embodies the house of the creator and mirrors the story of the struggle of darkness and light throughout time.

I was drawn to this temple because on many other occasions, during short visits on police-escorted caravans, I have had just a glimpse into its beauty and just a moment to experience the powerful energies here. More importantly, I was guided here by the Sirian High Council.

I believe that the Pharaoh Sety I still walks the halls and that his spirit is embodied in the temple, the grounds, and the holy city itself. In a way, I was drawn to follow the footsteps of Omm Sety, the extraordinary Dorothy Eady, whom you can read about in the work *The Search for Omm Sety,* to meet the past in the temple of Abydos and to ask the gods for guidance. A woman with an incredible connection to this sacred place, she communicated with Sety I for all of her life, which for the most part, she spent in the sacred halls of Abydos.

You mentioned that you would be aided and assisted by guardians and initiates. Who are they exactly?

I have always been blessed with the support of facilitators in all the work I have done for spirit. This has been accelerated since the first encounters with the Sirian High Council in the crop circle, the Julia Set, in 1996.

Inevitably and incredibly, everywhere events, people and forces appear to me who are willing to unlock the locked gates, to open closed doors, and to share the secrets that are needed at that point of my journey—at that initiation.

In the case of Abydos, there are people who prefer to be un-named so that they are protected, who have provided me access to secret spaces, underground tunnels, and sacred halls where it is not permitted by the government and by the Egyptian authorities.

I believe that they appear in service as I am to help bring the information out as is needed now and as part of their own spiritual process, and that this family of light is connected on many levels of consciousness. Whether fully aware of their role or not, they appear at the right time, the right place, and with the right intention—providing access to secret passageways for me and, in many cases, for those who travel with me. And I am grateful, so grateful to them, for their dedication, love and assistance.

You talked about unlocking the forces of Giza. What exactly is the plan?

The monuments at Giza and beyond the Plateau, to include the lesser pyramids and the step pyramid of Sakkara, are all located above a gigantic energy plant with its underground city, which is, topographically, far more immense than the surface urban city of Cairo. There are extensive tunnel networks, roadways, and structures there, and these are all related to the utilization of the Great Pyramid and its surrounding structures in the harnessing of cosmic energy.

We are becoming aware of the existence of multidimensional portals that lead through the dimensions, into other galaxies, other universes—and who knows where else. These portals are directly linked with the chakric centers and energy grids of Gaia herself. Of these, the epicenter is Giza; the entire plateau is a gateway. That is why the Sphinx was first created for us there.

That is why the Great Pyramids are there. And that is why the Atlantean record keepers left their imprint below.

While you still can, visit these locations with the intention to raise the vibration, reveal the secrets, play the music, and activate the stargates. This is the task of all of us—as starseed—and it begins with the most humble sense of service to the greater good.

Required now is an overwhelming need for heart-centered consciousness and the conviction that, despite the illusions of darkness, we know we are a breath away from the great shift, whereby a new world unfolds.

The obstructions are increasing, and it is becoming more difficult for so many people to release themselves from their fears and survival issues to truly dedicate to the bigger picture. This requires letting go of emotional issues and conditional love. It requires forgiveness and acceptance, and this, too, is asked of us now if we are to turn the wheels of Giza.

Be as clear as you can be of your own ego and how it wishes to distract you from the higher purpose, obscuring your focus, placing your personal experience and the manifestation of phenomena over the good of the entirety. It is time to dedicate our thoughts to the ultimate outcome, the highest good of all life, as the overriding collective consciousness—believing, at the individual level, that this is not only possible . . . it is our creation. The dissolution of the dark force is the natural outcome of our brilliant mind collective.

Does the work being done today have anything to do with the energies being put into place for the next couple of years or is it only preparation for 2012?

There is a battle of wills occurring now that is at its peak in Egypt. On the one hand, we have the forces who are attempting to block all access to the force fields of the sacred sites in order to lower the vibration of our planet. This is elaborated in the second book of the Sirian Revelations trilogy, *Atlantis Rising.*

On the other, we have untold numbers of dedicated Light-workers, joining forces around the world and linking in the ethers, to raise the frequencies of our planet in preparation for a new dawn: our ascension into the next realm.

Every thought and every action taking place across the Cosmos affects every other. There is one thing we are learning in our spiritual progression. It is that all is interconnected and that matter is thought, made manifest. The year 2009 is a time of preparation at the individual level. We are called to choose our locations and migrate there, so that we can feel empowered by those choices, rather than victimized by our circumstances. We are working with monumental energies, dedicating ourselves to the light, and this is as much a process of preparation as it our personal and civil responsibility as ancient souls who have chosen to take part in this process. And we are finally listening to our planet, seeking the answers that can calm the fury of our past and present negligence—to restore the balance. It is very important not to fixate on a given date, despite the markers we have been shown by the Mayans and other civilizations. We constantly change our reality—we saw this at the onset of the millennium, when so many people believed in an Armageddon situation at the turning of the clocks at midnight, December 31, 1999. What we need to hold in our hearts and minds is that we are moving toward a great awakening, that this process is so close we can feel it on every level, that we came to do this. 2009 brings us closer; 2012 closer still. But let us never forget that we create our reality and that we can intend that it be a smooth process, painless and without suffering, or we can fixate on disaster, loss, and tragedy.

I personally do not intend to suffer in any way the coming of this enormous event, and I declare that all you need to prepare is to reach into your heart and trust that all is in Divine Order. It sounds simplistic at times, as we search for detailed answers to the questions of our existence, but simple it is. All is in Divine Order, and we, children of the light, are on our way home.

Will there be many portals opening in Egypt in the years to come?

Interestingly enough, the more the forces of opposition try to close us out of the sacred sites, the more easily we access them on other levels. Egypt holds many gateways and vortices that lead us to our memory of Atlantis—and to its validation. These secrets are being withheld because the powers that hold rank in this plane do not want history to be rewritten. They do not want the veil to come down, revealing all the secrets that they have withheld.

And so, in a physical sense, many discoveries in Egypt and in other sacred lands are coming to light—all is coming into the light of our evolving consciousness. On other levels, as portals between dimensions or fields of consciousness, Egypt unquestionably holds many keys to our awakening. Below the Great Sphinx, Sirian effigy, lies the Atlantean Hall of Records.

Below the Osireion is located the etheric Master skull of the Skull Committee, which will be soon activated in Mayaland. The stargates of Egypt, I believe, will open the gates of the entire world.

Twenty-Two

THE CRYSTAL SKULLS, EXTRATERRESTRIAL VISITORS, AND CROP CIRCLES

Information circulating about the crystal skulls has been going on for a very long time. A lot of people claim to have one of the "original" skulls. Personally, I have heard many times that the thirteenth skull was found and could be in France or elsewhere. Today, we even have companies that make them, so everybody can have their own little crystal skull. I am not judging this commercial aspect, but to say the least, this could brings confusion between what is real what is not.

If possible, for clarification purposes, can you tell us in which countries are the skulls and whether they are in the hands of authentic keepers?

The reason you are hearing so much about the crystal skulls at this time has everything to do with their imminent reunion in the Mayalands, and all that that encompasses for Humankind. It is a primordial memory, a part of the collective consciousness of your species.

Many ancient Atlanteans are in body again at this time, having come to rectify the karma that was formed of their thoughts and actions. They hold the memory in their subconscious reservoirs, knowing, at the deepest levels, that the time of reunion is imminent. Indeed, many of these old souls have reincarnated now just to be there, among you, when this occurs.

As to the locations of the Atlantean skulls, we can tell you that only three have surfaced in your contemporary reality and that the other nine are in safekeeping, awaiting the time of convergence. The thirteenth, removed altogether from the density of the third dimension, exists in its etheric form below the Osireion in Egypt as mentioned by Trydjya [Patricia Cori]. It will be materialized at the time the others are joined together.

That so many are enthralled with the vibrational aspects of such modern carvings is, for some, inspired by memory and, for others, a projection into a moment when reunion will occur.

You are not the first generation to worship such forms— many others have before you! Ancient carvers have idolized the skull in crystal long before you—so powerful is the memory and the legend of the Skull Committee. Some of these old world skulls have reappeared now, and they have their imprints and codes. Some are incredible light fields; some are of the darkness—for the form itself is an exceptional container for the storing of information, while the conscious cellular units of the mineral respond to and hold the intention that activated it at any time in its journey.

Others have been created in these, your Earth days, and they, too, hold the intent and love of their modern-day sculptors. This is why it is so important, when working with such tools, that you clear all energies that are not of the highest intention. It is a mantra that you need if you intend to work with them.

Remember, dear one, that it is all *real*. Each experience and the thoughts that emanate from each moment are very real, indeed. It all serves to create the right dynamics for the convergence, for it focuses your minds out of limitation and onto the field of probabilities, which lies just ahead of you, just as it lies within every cell of your being.

You talk about the "Committee of Skull." How does the committee work together at this point without them being "together" and also without the master skull?

Each of the skulls of Atlantis, gifted from Sirius, carries the blueprint of *one* of your twelve light strands of DNA—the blueprint of the superrace of *Homo sapiens*. Each is a record keeper of the higher dimensional intelligence, which brought it to crystallize in your realm, holding all the frequencies and lightforms within it. Is it any wonder to you that they will be reunited at a time when you are reactivating the golden filaments of DNA? The reunion of the twelve, like the rewiring of your twelve strands, activates the Master. Let this serve you as an allegory for your own process.

United, the twelve crystal skulls manifest the original intention of the White Priesthood, that being the opening of the galactic portals at a time that enough of you, the collective mind, would have reached the vibrational frequencies to begin your ascension out of limitation.

When the twelve are united, the Master Skull of Osiris will be exhumed from its location and it will take form within the circle of twelve.

From what I heard and read, it seems that there are twelve skulls that are of feminine energy, and the thirteenth is of masculine energy. Is that so? If yes, what is the purpose in this?

There is no separate female or male quality to a member of the Skull Committee—this is a misconception. The sense of gender would be perhaps be borne of a psychic perception, on the part of the observer, of the Keeper who is currently acting as guardian of the skull.

We would like to add that our channel, Trydjya, lays no claim to the skull's origins other than its being gifted to her from its former guardian, the Mayan teacher and spirit guardian of the temples of Palenque, who gave her the name of the skull when he transferred guardianship to her.

Could we say that there is a subcommittee preparing the way for the great gathering of skulls that is planned for 2012?

[From Patricia]: Skulls are surfacing all over the world. Recently, about 150 shamans from Mayalands (I was supposed to go!) gathered at Tikal, and each had his or her skull there. We have skulls from Tibet, Nepal, other locations in the Himalayas, with the Native Americans, the Mayalands from Mexico to Peru, and others that are in the hands of contemporary keepers on other continents. At this time of our awakening, these skulls (some ancient, some contemporary) are coming into the foreground because they are the representations of the original thirteen skulls of Atlantis, gifted to Humankind by higher dimensional beings from Sirius and, as believed by the Mayans, some from the Pleiadies. All have their importance, for they represent that collective memory of all Human beings, of all time lines, of the Skull Committee and what it meant to Humanity (when we were *aware* of our galactic family and actively interacting). Now the one that is coming to me is very, very ancient—the Mayan skull, gifted by the shaman. I have no idea about its age, only that he has told me it is very, very old, comes from Egypt, and has been in his family for a long time. Shamans are always very vague about such things as the people who need to get the information, they believe, get it directly from the source—in this case, the skull itself.

Yes, I am very excited and honored to have now actually guardianship of three ancient skulls (there is a third one, small, of amethyst, that comes from Mexico near the temple of Atlantis Tula. I often bring the skulls in all the sacred sites with me, including the Great Pyramid, Stonehenge, Palenque, Chichen Itza, and the crop circles.

It seems that more and more we are visited by extraterrestrials spacecraft. Also, in November 2007, high-ranking officials from the military and the government from seven different countries have made public the fact that they witnessed spacecraft in the course of their work or on a personal level. Many countries have now released a lot of information concerning these visitations. It's out, and nothing is going to stop it. But, at the same time, there is a lot of information starting to get out concerning these contacts—that they do not always have our best interest at heart.

The spacecraft that we see—who are they, exactly?

As you pass through the photon belt, preparing for ascension, your solar body of planets, moons, and celestial bits and pieces are of great interest to alien explorers, corresponding to your own astrophysicists, engineers, geologists, and astronauts.

Beyond the question of the aliens already well entrenched in Earth affairs, as described in our earlier works, there is significant interest, from beyond your world, as to how you are going to evolve technologically and spiritually to make the transition.

There are absolutely lower-energy beings fascinated by the primitive forces of violent man, such as the Draconians, who feed off the lower vibrations of your species. They are involved in studies of the biological makeup of primary species on Earth with the intention of harvesting you (Humans and large primates) as warriors and slave networks. They are found hovering about your night skies, performing their examinations and tests on Human beings and animals. This is hardly "news," as thousands of individuals have reported abduction experiences, and others have witnessed animal mutilations. It simply isn't "mainstream" consciousness.

There are others, species from your sister planets, more concerned with the damage you are doing to your immediate galactic environment—your solar logos—and how you will affect their process of galactic ascension. They observe you, with no particular agenda, other than to evaluate the danger you pose and how to disarm you. They remain incredulous that you are still in the dark as to the existence of intelligent life there, on nearby worlds. Earth species live and reproduce on your moon—entire cities now thrive in biospheres constructed at the surface. On Mars, where your space rovers have traversed the planet for years, there exist extensive military and scientific bases at the surface and below—and these are manned by interplanetary hierarchies, which (it may surprise you to hear) include the Human race.

Increasingly, ambassadors from peaceful, evolved alien civilizations are probing your atmosphere and searching your skies to assure that the laws of noninterventionism are honored and that your welcome into the Galactic Family be one of wonder and celebration rather than one of trepidation and fear.

The Annunaki-led governments of your world, those who manipulate reality to conform to the policy of global control, know that the time of convergence is upon them and that they cannot delay the contact hour. Their secrets will be revealed, and the alien story will, at last, be known. They, too, fly the night skies. Their purpose, unfortunately, is to convince you that only they can save you from the ultimate terrorists: aliens from space.

What about the information that there is another group who is here for one reason, and that it is for their own purpose and that it has nothing to do with helping us or the great shift that is going on Earth at this time? They are here solely for commercial reasons because the planet Earth has many resources that are important to them. They are here to manipulate us into believing that they are here to help. They want to win the allegiance of Humanity and take away our independence. They do not wish to destroy but to utilize our resources, with or without our permission. They see the Earth like a very chaotic place and Humans as very undisciplined people destroying very important resources.

This point of view emanates from fear, which is being stirred up by the power that rules over you and exacerbated by way of their media channels. May we suggest that it is also a reflection of your own social behavior, a mirror of much of Humankind's detachment from nature and all that is conscious on your planet.

Is it not you, the most intelligent species on Earth, who are stripping your planet of its rich resources? Surely you are allowing the secret government to suck the life out of Gaia! Is it not the Human race that is creating the chaos, while you allow yourselves to be utilized to steal what is not yours to have, to kill in the name of peace and "holiness," and to destroy whatever stands in the way of "progress"?

Dear ones, we ask that you not give your power away to the idea that a benevolent, external force will sweep down and save you from yourselves. This is your karmic responsibility. Yes, there is a controlling force on your planet, that we do not deny, but the overall focus on material reality has, for too long, blinded you to the truth behind these realities and rendered you powerless—indeed, utterly disinterested—in changing your world for the better.

That you are seen as a destructive species is a partial truth. Those who observe you realize that despite the shadow forces that would bring Gaia to the lowest vibrational frequencies, there is an ever-growing circle of love and light encircling your planet. It is rippling out into the ethers, through your solar family and out into the galactic fields . . . even farther, through the Cosmos. What you connect with, in this polarized field of alien visitations, has everything to do with your own understanding of how you create your reality, how you take responsibility for your creations, and, hence, how you manifest what comes into your life in the illusion of the 3D realm.

Instead of being in fear, may we suggest you change your focus completely to read, *How can we communicate our intention to the intelligence intent upon connecting with the Human race so that we send messages of love and nonviolence instead of fear and retaliation?*

As you increasingly understand the law of attraction, you will realize that it is you who will determine how this plays out in your world. The more you assist each other to release yourselves from the irrational fear being stirred within you by the extremely violent portrayal of Earth besieged, the more joyful you will feel over the prospect of what is about to occur. That joy and serenity will create a resonant field—a melody—with those who seek harmony between all beings. Discernment begins with your own self-examination of how you create and live in illusion, and how you can transmute the fear into anticipation.

So at this time, the purpose is mainly to be "seen," so we can get used to them?

You will see incredible numbers of craft in these days as you rapidly approach the hour of global contact. In fact, it has already begun. There is so much activity just above your heads, just as there is below your feet. Were you to see the Earth as we do, you would be amazed at what travels the airways and outer atmosphere of your planet. We note that it is the tendency of the Human race to blind itself to what lies beyond those fields of possibility that have been constructed by those who wish you to look no further.

In truth, there are craft perpetually roaming above you—exploring, studying, and analyzing how contact should be organized—and there exist galactic laws that must be respected. Observing how you can be manipulated not to see what is clearly in front of you, we believe that you will only "get used to" visiting craft when your skies are so irrevocably filled with their lights that you can no longer be convinced they are not there.

There is a crop circle that appeared at West Kennett on July 26 that some have called the three faiths—*the Islam, Jewish, and Christian faiths (see picture). Can you tell us what is the meaning of this crop circle? Is it a message telling us that in the future all religions will coexist together without problem? Is it a sign for the future?*

The crop lay in question was made of Human hands, and so our comments would be based on our interpretation, rather than our intent. It speaks not to us of your collective yearning to release from separation, exasperated by the misinterpretation of religions and experience unity of heart, mind and soul. Rather, we observe:

- the circle: the All, the One, the Monad, the Atum;
- the pentagram: Spirit—the five elements that define the nature of Earth reality contained within the All: air, water, fire, earth, and ethos;
- the cross: the intersection point of the vertical axis (spirit-being-earth), linking you to the earth and heavens,

and the horizontal axis, your passage in the 3D illusion of linear time.

These unite to speak of your existence within the physical reality, your ability to manipulate the elements, which define your earthly condition and your understanding of how, as sparks of the divine light, you are reflections of the *All That Is, That Ever Was, and Forever Will Be.* It is the intent of the designer who sends a message through symbol, and it is the receptive mind of the receiver to give the archetypes meaning to his or her own life. So, we ask you to find your own truth there and make meaning of the message, connecting to the intent behind it.

I was very surprised to hear that this crop circle was manmade. Is this something that happens very often? Is it important to know which ones are manmade and which ones that are interdimensional?

What excites those of us beyond your realm is that Human hands, hearts, and minds are dedicated to respond to the cosmometric messages of extradimensional origins. We are communicating in the only true universal language!

We send our many messages intent on initiating a global dialogue—what else would be the purpose of it all? To merely impress you with our artistic references? Would you consider this to be for the highest good of All? No, indeed not. Rather, we wish to stir you to look beyond the boundaries of your realm. Without your response, there is no dialogue, and our intention is to open communication lines between the Human race and the greater galactic family.

So it is that we celebrate those crop designs (of the Human hand) as the intent to communicate, rather than to deceive. To those Human circle makers who spend hours in the cold night, tracing (however rudimentarily) their geometric forms into the fields, intent on communicating beauty and the meaning of sacred form, to them we send our gratitude and love.

Our hearts are filled with the messages, the intent, and the commitment that crop circles bring to the phenomenon of multidimensional communication. And so are theirs. Is there really a difference between the two experiences? Is any one of these any more significant than any other?

Then I will ask about another one that was magnificent. It was a butterfly that appeared July 19, 2007, near Ashbury. Was this one from interdimensional intention or again manmade? I wonder because butterflies are very "hot" these days. We see this symbol everywhere—in photographs, pictures, decorative items, and so on. It seems to reflect our spiritual journey.

It is not manmade. We speak to you of vibration, frequency, and attunement. The symbol—the sphere carried in the wings—is a metaphor for Gaia, carried along the vibrations of the One Soul. It is intended as a message for you, starseeds, to understand how the smallest movement—a flutter of wings—can alter the entirety. From the chrysalis (the dark cocoon) to the wing, so is our passage.

Always remember how every thought, of every living being, contributes to the Cosmos of Soul. And fly, dear one—fly on the wings of love.

What information is the most important to know before entering the year 2009?

You are now in the Desert Days of extreme polarity, to which we have dedicated much reflection in earlier messages. You are in the process of cracking apart your material world while Gaia, wise mother, pushes you to the extremes. She is tossing you about, flooding you with emotion, blowing down your illusions so that you recognize how the material focus of your world is as impermanent as autumn leaves.

In this context of linear time, the last six lunar cycles of the solar year, your fears of survival will be tested with more extreme weather patterns, political and social instability, and further economic uncertainty.

You will be confronted with conditions that guide you either upward, along that vertical axis of spirit over matter, or downward, where you cling to your possessions, symbols of your focus on limitation and the search for permanence in an impermanent world. It is your decision, and yours alone, of just how much you intend to suffer as Gaia's cracks the shell of her mortal existence and cleanses her physical frame for rites of passage into her immortal light body. For those of you whose focus is on the peaceful progression of the One Heart on the spiral of consciousness, a great sense of Unity will illuminate your passage through the valleys of turmoil and darkness. As you share your insights and experience, you create such brilliant fields of light that your fears of the shadow fade into oblivion. In the dynamics of astro-physical cosmometry, your galaxy is preparing a most exquisite alignment as Earth's axis shifts and leans toward the galactic plane, which has been defined by your astrologers as the "Holy Cross." This celestial field manifested mid-June 2008, marking a phenomenal point of evolutionary acceleration for Earth and all life on the surface and deep within the inner worlds.

It is the astro-marker on the time-space continuum that heralds your progression from the extremes of the duality consciousness to the merging of the male/female aspects—the Unification of the polar extremes—of your societies and your souls.

The last Holy Cross alignment to occur in your galaxy was the time of the Great Flood, at that time that you recognize as the sinking of Atlantis, where the darkness was purified in the waters of Gaia and the new was birthed.

I think it's important to take further this information about this unusual astrological alignment that contains the potential of a phenomenal point of evolution acceleration for Earth and all life on the surfaces because the last time that this kind of alignment occurred was the sinking of Atlantis. How will we be affected?

We have consistently pointed the way of liberation and transition as beginning through the purified heart, where you experience unconditional love and fearlessness. In a sense, the heart is of itself a holy cross, for it is the intersection point of the higher and lower energies and the epicenter of the left and right alignments of your own physical forms.

There are many climactic moments of transition lying before you, and all are facilitated by your focused intent to release yourselves from those emotional traps and conditions that provoke feelings of unworthiness, suffering, intolerance, and guilt. These, in the purified heart, transmute into unconditional love and forgiveness, which are one and the same.

Your choice is to clear yourselves of these imbalances now or to hold onto the drama of your suffering: your dark cloak of unresolved emotion and karma. This is the process that determines not only your passage through the Holy Cross alignment, but how you live every day of your lives. It is the only measure of your preparation. Are you willing to love yourselves and all others simply because they exist—in divine order—or will you spend the rest of your time in body demanding that the universe conform to the conditions you place before yourself?

To forgive yourselves and others for all that creates disharmony in your experience and to replace that imbalance with a deep understanding of how the choice is yours to make are the simplest of guidelines to the pathway of your passage. Fear and the need to somehow control the outcome are your deterrents.

When you contemplate the true magnificence of your Earth, and the perpetual birthing of life, you let go of the paralysis that fear brings. You look to the stars, knowing the Divine Plan is in perfect order and wonder, rather than fear, what incredible leaps you are destined for.

Your preparation lies in your surrender—letting go, letting God.

Twenty-Three

BEYOND 2009: THE DESERT DAYS

From the High Council's perspective, what does the nest few years hold for us? Since this book's title is The Great Shift, *how can we better prepare for what is coming?*

The process of preparation for the immensity of the celestial shifts on the outer plane is to prepare yourselves, at the cellular or inner plane, for the cleansing of toxic consciousness (manifesting as matter), which you have formed by clinging to the density of judgment, separation, and ego—and surrendering to the unconditional love that underlies the Cosmos.

No matter how remote that love can seem at times, it pervades all things. To this end, we remind you that you either believe in God, Prime Creator, or you do not. If you do, then inherent in that belief you must realize that all that occurs is the conscious stream of God Mind. From the darkness of the most difficult hours and the shadows of lost souls, to the brilliance of the dawn, the glitter of angels, all is in Divine Order.

To facilitate the process of your transmutation from the density to the light, learning to experience the unfolding events in serenity and acceptance, you must seek the spiritual understanding of life and your time in body.

Practical methods include removing, as much as you possibly can, all toxic conditions from your environment and all toxic thoughts from your fields of consciousness. The first is accomplished by

• reducing all electromagnetic devices, which interfere with your natural energy flows and biorhythms;

• replacing synthetic clothing, food, and chemicals from your environments with natural fibers, wholesome vegetarian food, and organic substances;

• drinking of purified water, rearranged at the cellular level through your conscious thoughts, prayer, and meditations—and the application of sacred geometrical forms;

• selecting harmonious environments with the best air quality, soils, and attunement with nature;

• exercising your physical bodies to remain vigorous while breathing in prana for the illumination of every cellular unit.

The second is accomplished through

• meditation and proper breathing;

• consciously choosing forgiveness over revenge, tolerance over judgment, love over hate, trust over fear;

• surrendering to unconditional love by loving unconditionally;

• confronting and accepting your emotions by bringing them to the full light of consciousness before releasing them through your heart centers and into the Earth to be healed;

• spending time in nature, loving animals, smelling clean air, breathing in the splendor of the trees, the flowers—the gifts of Eden;

• seeking beauty and taking the time to celebrate all that is right in your world;

• avoiding those of the lower vibration who wish to entrain you in their negative thoughts and actions;

• intending, in all of your thoughts and actions, that only the highest good be served.

Now is the time to take yourselves to the sacred sites of the Earth, for there you will feel the energies of the Earth, of the ancients who worshipped there, of others like you who bring your love and light to these vortices. You will experience powerful shifts and acceleration in your energy bodies, particularly in this time following the manifestation of the Holy Cross (June 2008), and your experience will be one of unity and connection to Gaia.

Create altars to Spirit, however you worship, respecting the wisdom underlying the cosmometry of form and consciousness, the vibration of the vertical axis (spirit-being Earth) and the power of the horizontal plane to create a place where you are able to find the absolute epicenter of your own existence.

We would like to end our participation in this project by saying that what you need most, at this time of radical change, is a doctrine of "right thought" that will allow you to focus on what you already have, what you already know, and what, most importantly, you have co-created with Gaia, your immensely powerful and loving mother. If you ask yourselves what you are feeling overwhelmed about, in the calm of your centered minds and balanced emotional bodies, you cannot but realize that your fear is of the unknown—of anything that lurks outside your comfort zones and those illusory "safety" nets that the power continually throw over your conscious awareness of what is truly occurring in your world.

You are marketed and maneuvered into feeling powerless and afraid of the most insignificant things, when you think about it! Won't you agree that it is becoming more of a challenge to merely exit your front doors?

We say to you, however desperate the events may seem to you, it is all part of your process of awakening. Pay attention but observe with detachment what goes around you. Be centered, stilling the lower emotions. Be wary and look carefully about you, turning your focus away from the horror and toward beauty, love, and miracles that surround you in every moment of your lives. Above all, starseed, you do well to remember that you chose to be here. You chose it, fully aware of the hills and valleys of your passage.

Now is the time to remember, dear children of light and beauty.

Now is the time to remember who you truly are.

We hold you in our hearts and mind.

We are the Sirian High Council.

ABOUT THE CONTRIBUTORS

LEE CARROLL has been channeling Kryon for more than twenty years and is the author of over eleven Kryon books, most recently *Lifting the Veil: The New Energy Apocalypse*. Lee and his spiritual partner, Jan Tober, started the "Kryon light groups" in 1991 and quickly moved from a living room setting to a Del Mar, CA church. Now they are hosting meetings all over the globe with audiences of up to 3,000 people. In the beginnings of the Internet, Kryon had the largest consistent New Age folder in the history of America Online and the Kryon site still receives over 20,000 visits a day. Carroll is also the co-author of *The Indigo Children*.

TOM KENYON is a teacher, scientist, sound healer, shaman, and psychotherapist. He is also a channel for Mary Magdalene and for the Hathors, interdimensional beings who are masters of love and sound from an ascended intergalactic civilization. His books include *The Hathor Material* and *The Magdalen Manuscript*.

PATRICIA CORI is a highly regarded clairvoyant/channel, spiritual guide, and master teacher and the author of a series of books of the Sirian Revelations, including *No More Secrets, No More Lies: A Handbook to Starseed Awakening*, plus *The Cosmos of Soul: A Wake-Up Call For Humanity* and *Atlantis Rising: The Struggle of Darkness and Light*.

ABOUT THE EDITOR

MARTINE VALLÉE, who collected this volume and originally published it in French, is the publisher of Ariane Editions, French language publishers of such best-selling authors as Eckhart Tolle, Esther and Jerry Hicks, Gregg Braden, and Drunvalo Melchizedek.

TO OUR READERS

Weiser Books, an imprint of Red Wheel/Weiser, publishes books across the entire spectrum of occult and esoteric subjects. Our mission is to publish quality books that will make a difference in people's lives without advocating any one particular path or field of study. We value the integrity, originality, and depth of knowledge of our authors.

Our readers are our most important resource, and we appreciate your input, suggestions, and ideas about what you would like to see published. Please feel free to contact us, to request our latest book catalog, or to be added to our mailing list.

Red Wheel/Weiser, LLC
500 Third Street, Suite 230
San Francisco, CA 94107
www.redwheelweiser.com